TEENAGE REBELS

SUCCESSFUL HIGH SCHOOL ACTIVISTS FROM THE
LITTLE ROCK 9 TO THE CLASS OF TOMORROW

Dawson Barrett

table of CONTENTS

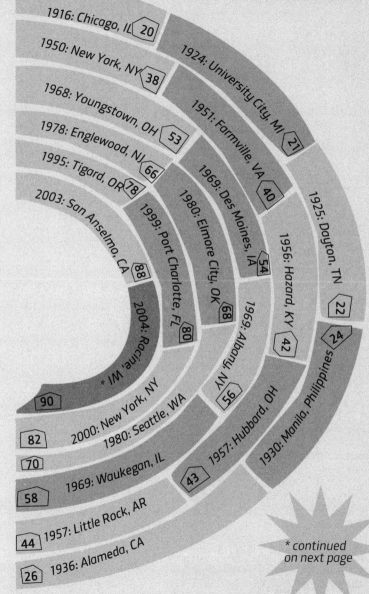

1916: Chicago, IL [20]

1924: University City, MI

1950: New York, NY [38]

1951: Farmville, VA [27]

1968: Youngstown, OH [53]

1969: Des Moines, IA [40]

1925: Dayton, TN [22]

1978: Englewood, NJ [66]

1956: Hazard, KY

1995: Tigard, OR [78]

1980: Elmore City, OK [54]

2003: San Anselmo, CA [88]

1999: Port Charlotte, FL [80]

1969: Albany, NY [68]

1956: Hazard, KY [42]

2004: Racine, WI * [90]

1930: Manila, Philippines [24]

2000: New York, NY [82]

1980: Seattle, WA [70]

1969: Albany, NY [56]

1957: Hubbard, OH [43]

1969: Waukegan, IL [58]

1957: Little Rock, AR [44]

1936: Alameda, CA [26]

* continued
on next page

5

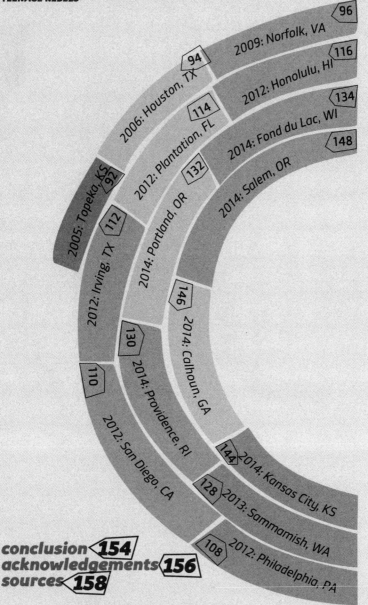

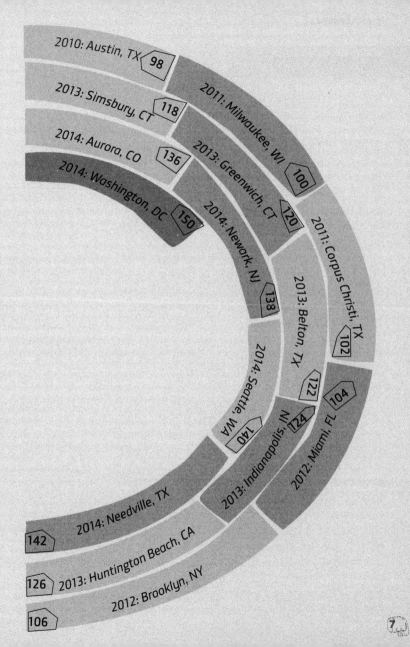

2010: Austin, TX 98

2011: Milwaukee, WI 100

2011: Corpus Christi, TX 102

2012: Miami, FL 104

2012: Brooklyn, NY 106

2013: Simsbury, CT 118

2013: Greenwich, CT 120

2013: Belton, TX 122

2013: Indianapolis, IN 124

2013: Huntington Beach, CA 126

2014: Aurora, CO 136

2014: Newark, NJ 138

2014: Seattle, WA 140

2014: Needville, TX 142

2014: Washington, DC 150

FOREWORD

By Mark Rudd

My own teenage career seemed like an interminable waiting room: I knew my life would begin once I went to college. And that's exactly what happened. In 1965, as a freshman at Columbia University, I immediately fell in with a group of students who wanted to change the world, the Columbia chapter of Students for a Democratic Society, SDS. I joined with them in helping to build the student movement to end the war in Vietnam and institutional racism; we were part of much bigger social and political movements at the time. In retrospect I now see what was missing from my high school years—involvement in the real world. SDS was precisely what I had been waiting for.

The very term **"teenager"** is so new in our language that it's got to be suspect. Amazingly, it seems to have arisen right after World War II as a mass marketing scheme: first you identify a new age niche—with built-in insecurities and worries about being cool—then you sell the newly created "teenagers" billions of dollars of stuff. The term caught on with lightning speed only seventy years ago. (I was born in 1947 and grew up assuming that the word had always existed). But the next logical question is "How did people between the ages of twelve and nineteen behave before 'teenagers' were invented?"

The best I can figure out is that in most societies throughout most of history, including the U.S. before 1945, people spent their teen years learning how to be adults. Since so much of the world's population was and still is rural and agrarian, child farmwork is a given, to help the family. But even in 20th century industrial societies such as the U.S., kids of a certain age were expected to either go to work or go to school, which was the path to an adult life of work. One can imagine that these choices for people who would later be called "teenagers" were pretty serious.

The great thing about this book you're setting out to read is that it cuts through the strange separateness, superficiality, and social disconnectedness commonly ascribed to teenagers to the underlying core truth that teens are people who are connected to their world. Every single astonishing story that Dawson relates—from sixteen-year-old Sybil Ludington's 1777 ride to alert the militia of a British attack to the 21st century high school students fighting for gay and transgender rights and the rights of immigrants—illustrate the deep concern of young people about their society, and their willingness to act on that.

Above all, young people have time and again shown their ability to imagine a better and more just world.

Even if they choose to ignore them, most teenagers are aware of the great interrelated crises facing us: constant war and militarization, economic and political inequality, the persistence of racism and poverty, the looming ecological disaster of man-made global warming facing the planet. What to do in response is not immediately obvious because the tradition of protest has almost been extinguished. But as mass movements such as the immigration Dreamers and the opposition to continuing reliance on fossil fuels grow, the examples of high school kids organizing in *Teenage Rebels* will serve as useful models and a spur to further study and action. It's your world; I'm planning to check out pretty soon (though I'll continue to organize 'til then).

A note about your author: I first met Dawson almost 10 years ago when he was about to leave Portland, Oregon to move to Milwaukee, Wisconsin to work on his doctorate in history. Dawson was a hardcore punk rocker who was putting together a punk rock festival as his goodbye present to his adopted city. Knowing of my ancient history as a college student organizer and later "revolutionary," Dawson invited me to speak to Steal This Festival. We had a blast, as 200 people talked between bands about the underlying problems of society and how to organize. A few years later I visited him at the University of Wisconsin-Milwaukee where he had organized an extremely active chapter of the new SDS. In recent years I've learned an awful lot from reading and discussing with Dawson his doctoral dissertation on the cultural and political responses to the post-Sixties crisis of Neo-Liberalism (the form of global capitalism that we have in the world). Among the many responses he described was. . . punk rock activism! So you're in good hands for the next 150 pages. Enjoy these stories. They're historical avatars for a new era, one in which kids will most likely choose reality over reality TV, since it's so much cooler. And the best of all is imagining a new world.

INTRODUCTION

In 1962, college students in Michigan drafted a political manifesto called the Port Huron Statement. "We are people of this generation," they proclaimed, "looking uncomfortably to the world we inherit." They modeled their group, Students for a Democratic Society, after the civil rights organizations of high school and college students that had been coordinating sit-ins and other protests in the American South. By the late 1960s, SDS had become a leading student voice against racism and war, with hundreds of chapters on college campuses all over the country—and in many high schools as well. The high school activists, however, were not interested in taking orders from their older peers. As they saw it, navigating a high school was an entirely different task than a university, and no one understood the complexities of their surroundings better than they did.

Indeed, the teenagers' place in American society is full of contradictions and unusual challenges. In addition to the pressures of their home and work lives—and the often cruel treatment they receive from one another—teens also face a constant barrage of corporate advertising. American teenagers are a roughly 200 billion consumer market, and business' attempts to tap into those funds have had dramatic impacts on fashion, music, leisure, political opinions, and other aspects of youth culture.

At times, rebellious young people have pushed back against these efforts, by forming their own countercultures. Today, products influenced by punk rock, rap, skateboarding, graffiti writing, and break-dancing are available at any shopping mall, if not Wal-Mart and Target. The "cool" factor of rebel culture is a moneymaker for multi-national corporations, but these activities and ideas were originally forged by youth in the 1970s and 1980s. They were attempts by young people to carve out a small part of their lives that they could control, and for bucking authority, teenage rebels routinely suffered harassment, arrests, beatings, or worse. But there was no pure, authentic "back in the day." Youth countercultures are alive and well, and they are constantly evolving. Their survival is a testament to how brilliantly young people find fault in the assumptions of the ruling generation.

Most pertinent to this book, teenagers also face a variety of structural challenges in their specific roles as high school students. Chief among them is that the people who make the decisions that shape their educational experiences (for example, which books they will read, how much funding will go to their schools, who their classmates will be, and what their dress code standards will be) are not politically accountable to them. Some of these decisions are made by teachers. Others are made by teachers' bosses: principals, superintendents, and other administrators. Still, other policies are determined by government officials at various levels. District school boards and city councils typically set local policies, while state-level governments decide on budgets and common curricula. Federal officials, meanwhile, set national education policies (Congress), rule on the constitutionality of laws (the U.S. Supreme Court), and enforce those decisions (the President). High schoolers cannot vote for any of these people, but they can influence their policies in other ways.

This book is full of examples of high school students using whatever means available to them to try to shape their worlds by influencing people in power. In some cases, students opposed their teachers. In others, they defended teachers in clashes with administrators. In still other cases, students joined forces with both teachers and principals as they took on school boards, mayors, and other government officials. Sometimes, simply being organized was enough for students to make changes in their schools. Some policies existed not because anyone specifically opposed a change, but because no one had ever tried to make it. For example, many schools adopted recycling programs when students said they wanted them. In other cases, however, students encountered substantial resistance and employed various means of protest.

Throughout U.S. history, activists have conducted "sit-ins" in places where they were not allowed to sit, whether at racially segregated lunch counters or in the offices of politicians. These actions deliberately broke the rules and thus caused disruptions. In the most successful cases, the disruptions put pressure on the people who claimed to control those spaces. But since the main requirement for students is that they sit in their classrooms, the most logical (and popular) method of protest has been to do the exact opposite, to refuse to cooperate and walk out of school.

The effectiveness of these protests has varied. While almost always successful as an expression of dissent and disapproval, "walk-outs" have only occasionally resulted in students winning their demands. This was primarily because the people in power (the people who could give students what they wanted) are not always vulnerable to protests. Powerful people (principals and mayors, for example) try very hard to make protestors' actions and demands appear silly, immature, and otherwise inappropriate. For example, during a student protest in Fresno, Califaornia in 1936, the school principal discounted a massive walk-out as nothing more than a prank—a few misbehaving students playing "hooky." When this type of narrative was successful, parents and other community members agreed that students should return to class or face repercussions. Students became isolated, and they lost.

However, when students gained the support of teachers, parents, the courts, or community members (and were disruptive enough), they very often won. A week before the Fresno protests, students in Alameda, California challenged a decision made by their mayor. But rather than taking him on by themselves, students also secured the backing of his political opponents, which translated to positive coverage in the local newspaper, funds from local businesses, and the support of other government officials. These alliances made the difference, and the students won.

This book is not an attempt to demonstrate that teenagers have always been right or that they have always done the right thing. It may have been easier to put together examples of high school students being awful to one other and reinforcing the oppressive relationships of broader American society. For example, in the 1950s and 1960s, there were many white student protests against racial integration. Likewise, today's media accounts include essentially infinite examples of teenage bullying. The easiest book to write would have simply documented cases in which teenage rebellion has taken the form of self-destruction. But—and I believe this is important—high schoolers have often aimed their frustrations in the right direction—at the people who make the rules.

Despite immense social pressures and severe limitations on their political rights, teenagers have routinely tried to make the world around them just a little bit better. This book includes many such examples, and it is by no means exhaustive. In fact, I left out more than 100 of the cases that

I found, and I barely scratched the surface with my research. If your high school is not in this book, it probably could have been. High school students have been integral to every American social movement in the last hundred years, and they have almost always been ahead of the curve.

This is a book about fighting against the status quo to demand freedom, equality, and justice.

It is a book about not just breaking the rules, but challenging their very legitimacy.

This is a book about young people trying to shape the world they inherit.

1777: THE MIDNIGHT RIDE OF...
SYBIL LUDINGTON
Kent, New York

Teenagers have been integral to the political struggles of the United States since even before the country's founding. Many teens participated in the American Revolutionary War, and they did so for a variety of reasons. Some were interested in the independence of the colonies. Most, however, fought for their own freedom. They enlisted to escape poverty, or in hopes of escaping slavery or indentured servitude.

*One famous **teenage revolutionary** was Sybil Ludington.*

After British troops attacked Danbury, Connecticut in April 1777, a messenger was sent to request assistance from Colonel Henry Ludington. The members of Colonel Ludington's militia, however, were scattered, as they had been sent home to their farms for the spring planting season.

Contributors To The Cause...

U.S.

8c

Sybil Ludington

Youthful Heroine

As the colonel made preparations, his sixteen-year-old daughter Sybil rode her horse through the night, spreading word of the attack and gathering the soldiers under her father's command. The ride was dangerous. In addition to the darkness and the rain, she also risked encounters with British troops, their Loyalist supporters, and everyday thieves along her path.

From that evening into the next morning, Sybil Ludington covered about forty miles—roughly double that of Paul Revere's much more famous ride.

In 1975, she was featured on a U.S. postage stamp, and a statue in her honor stands in Carmel, New York.

1836: THE FACTORY GIRLS ASSOCIATION
Lowell, Massachusetts

In the 1820s, factory owners in Lowell, Massachusetts began recruiting the daughters of New England farmers to work in their textile mills. The "Lowell Mill girls," some as young as ten years old, slept six to a room in the company's dormitories and began their thirteen-hour work days at 5 a.m.

In 1834, mill owners announced that they would be cutting already meager wages by 15 percent. In response, workers held a series of meetings to discuss how they should respond. When owners fired one of their leaders, 800 young women walked out of the factory in one of the first industrial strikes in U.S. history.

Two years later, management announced yet another major wage cut, and more than 1,000 young women shut down the factory by marching out together. They formed a group called the "Factory Girls Association" and refused to interact with owners except through their chosen representatives.

The members of the Factory Girls Association viewed themselves as an extension of the country's revolutionary spirit, announcing, "As our fathers resisted unto blood the lordly avarice of the British ministry, so we, their daughters, never will wear the yoke that has been prepared for us." Though the strike failed after a month, the Lowell Mill girls' defiance was an inspiration to others.

For the next hundred years, labor clashes were among the defining political events in the industrializing United States. Through thousands of protests, strikes, and other work stoppages, workers demanded better working conditions, better pay, and the right to form labor unions (to have a say in workplace rules and policies). Until federal laws banning child labor became the norm in the 1930s, American teenagers worked alongside adults in the country's factories and mines, and they participated in many of the labor struggles that shaped the country's history. Their protests notably included the 1909 "Uprising of 20,000" in New York City, yet another strike by young women in American clothing factories.

17

1879: BOARDING SCHOOL RUNAWAYS
Carlisle Indian Industrial School //
Carlisle, Pennsylvania

By the mid-1800s, U.S. westward expansion included an extremely violent program to undermine American Indian nations' treaty rights and to force them off of their land. Many white Americans viewed indigenous people as racially inferior and a barrier to human progress (and a barrier to building gold mines on their land). With this task largely accomplished by the late 1870s, a U.S. Army Captain named Richard Henry Pratt proposed a new approach for the government's Indian policy.

In 1879, Pratt opened the Carlisle Indian Industrial School, an off-reservation boarding school for American Indian children. Pratt believed that American Indians were culturally inferior to European Americans, but that they could be "saved" through education. Adopting a slogan that he had to "kill the Indian" in order to "save the man," Pratt insisted that he could transform American Indian children into "real" Americans if he removed them from their communities.

At Carlisle, Pratt and the teachers forced students to cut their hair and to abandon traditional clothing in favor of military uniforms. The school forbade students from using their native languages and required them to speak exclusively in English. They also made students adopt new "American" names and required them to practice Christianity. Carlisle was located at the site of former military barracks, and officials enforced their rules using strict military-style discipline, with punishments ranging from hard labor to solitary confinement. The school quickly became a model for the federal government's American Indian policies, and the U.S. established 25 similar schools by the turn of the century. However, while Carlisle taught its students to be obedient workers (including through summer programs that "allowed" them to be domestic workers in white homes), the school produced very few graduates. According to one estimate, of the many thousands of students who attended Carlisle in its first twenty-four years, only 158 graduated.

Student rebellion at such boarding schools was common. Some students refused to answer to their newly assigned names. Others secretly practiced their religion or spoke in their native languages when not being watched by teachers. In at least one case, students sent a petition to the U.S. government requesting the closing of their school.

The most common form of resistance, however, was running away. In fact, "desertion" at the schools, by boys and girls alike, was so widespread that schools had to request that train employees refuse American Indian youth as passengers and offer cash rewards in neighboring towns for help with their return. According to historian Brenda Child, one frequent runaway from the Flandreau School in South Dakota was caught (in a single year during the early 1930s) in "Elkton, South Dakota, in Wilmar, Pipestone, and Minneapolis, Minnesota, and in Chicago, Illinois." The fifteen-year-old was otherwise considered a well-behaved student.

Deserters often received help from American Indian communities in reservations near schools, who protested government policy by providing sanctuary to runaways.

BEFORE

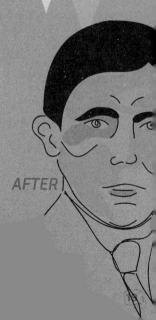

AFTER

1913: *THE SILENT ASSEMBLY*
Stuyvesant High School //
New York, New York

"VOCAL CORDS SILENT IN HIGH SCHOOL 'STRIKE'—BREAK DOWN DOOR ALSO"

In May 1913, a "large majority" of Stuyvesant High's 2,500 students refused to sing "America" at the school's morning assembly. Their silence was a protest against the school's lunchtime policy, which required students to stay in the building during their short noon break and to purchase lunch from the cafeteria, if they had not brought food from home.

At lunchtime that day, thirty-two students also "forced the doors" and enjoyed a half-hour of freedom before returning to school for the rest of their classes.

As the boys told the New York Tribune, students at other area high schools were allowed to "eat their luncheons where they wish and enjoy liberty during the noonday intermission" and they sought only "to assert what they believe to be their rights." The students also disparaged the quality of the school cafeteria's offerings.

Principal Ernest Von Nardroff defended the quality of the school's lunches and dismissed the strike as "nothing more than the individual opinions of a few dissatisfied boys." After all, he noted, every school had a certain number of students who "fancied grievances and who were restless and dissatisfied."

"JAMES E. BAKER FOR PRINCIPAL"

"WE WANT A SQUARE DEAL FOR BAKER"

In May 1924, after hearing that their principal's contract would not be renewed for the following school year, more than 200 students at University City High School paraded through the streets of St. Louis, Missouri carrying supportive signs and demanding his re-hiring.

Around noon, the march reached the school, where students gathered in the auditorium. Principal Baker thanked the protestors for their support and asked them to return to class for the remainder of the day. After several cheers of support, the students agreed to his request.

1925: THE BUTLER ACT & THE "TRIAL OF THE CENTURY"
Rhea County High School // Dayton, Tennessee

"It shall be unlawful for any teacher in any of the...public schools...to teach any theory that denies the story of the divine creation of man as taught in the Bible."

On March 21, 1925, Tennessee Governor Austin Peay signed into law the Butler Act, which outlawed the teaching of evolution in Tennessee's public schools. To challenge the new law, civil liberties activists began looking for a test case—someone who had broken it. John Scopes, a popular 24-year-old football coach and substitute science teacher at Rhea County High School, volunteered. Though he confessed that he could not actually remember whether or not he had covered evolution in his classes, he had used a (state-approved) textbook that included it. Scopes recruited students to testify against him, and he was formally indicted in May, facing a fine of several hundreds of dollars. Superintendent Walter White testified against Scopes, confirming that he had used the textbook and describing him as "a good teacher."

When the trial began, the teaching of evolution had been outlawed in the public schools of Oklahoma, Florida, and Texas, and similar laws were being considered in eleven other states. The story of Adam and Eve from the

Book of Genesis was promoted in its place, and the teaching of the Biblical story was actually required by law in Alabama, New Jersey, Pennsylvania, Tennessee, Georgia, and Mississippi.

The State of Tennessee v. John Thomas Scopes quickly became a major spectacle, making Dayton, Tennessee "famous overnight." Journalists from all over the country flooded the town. Christian conservatives rallied to support the prosecution, while scientists and civil liberties advocates backed the defense. Famously, three-time Presidential candidate William Jennings Bryan volunteered to argue for Tennessee, and prominent civil liberties attorney Clarence Darrow defended Scopes.

Though the Scopes "Monkey Trial" is very well known, less well known is that John Scopes lost. The jury was not allowed to assess the law itself, and they easily found him guilty of violating it (which he had not denied). On appeal, the Tennessee Supreme Court ruled that the Butler law had nothing at all to do with endorsing religion. However, they also dismissed the case on a technicality, in order to quash further public attention.

The Butler Law remained in effect in Tennessee until 1967, when it was challenged by Gary Scott, a science teacher at Jacksboro High School, after he was fired for teaching evolution. The next year, the U.S. Supreme Court ruled that similar laws in states all over the U.S. were unconstitutional because they violated the First Amendment rights of teachers.

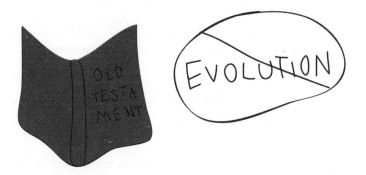

1930: "*10,000 STUDENTS STRIKE; OPPOSE U.S. TEACHER*" *Manila North High School // Manila, Philippines*

After the Spanish-American War in 1898, the United States abandoned its mission to liberate the former Spanish colonies of Puerto Rico, Cuba, Guam, and the Philippines and instead took them over. Maintaining control of the Philippines involved a very bloody war in which thousands of U.S. soldiers and many times as many Filipino soldiers and civilians were killed—and in which the United States used both torture and concentration camps. The Philippines then became an American colony, and remained so until after World War II.

As part of its imperial project in the Philippines, the U.S. government established several American primary and secondary schools. By 1921, Manila High School had grown so large that it split into Manila North and Manila South. In 1923, Manila East opened, followed by Legarda High (which later became Manila West).

In February 1930, after holding a mass meeting, roughly 2,700 students at Manila North High School walked out of school to demand the removal of their American teacher, Mabel Brummitt of Valparaiso, Indiana. According to the students, Brummitt had made racist comments about Filipinos, calling them "imbeciles." Said one student, Brummitt "time and again has branded Filipinos as savages, imbeciles, idiots, and contemptible cads." Brummitt, however, claimed she had been misunderstood, and that by misbehaving, one of the students was acting like "an imbecile."

As the protest became a proxy battle between the U.S. and local governments, the mayor of Manila told the students that he would be the first to lead them in a strike if Brummitt was allowed to return. The students won their demand, and Brummitt was removed, pending an investigation into her statements. However, school officials also expelled four of the strike's student leaders.

North High students again walked out to demand the reinstatement of their four classmates. This time, their ranks swelled to 10,000 strong, as students from Manila West, Manila South, and Manila East joined them.

The growing strike's demands also expanded to include the removal of the secretary of public education, the director of education, and the North High principal.

Seven students were arrested during the protests.

Alejandro Albert, the secretary of public education, threatened to expel all 10,000 of the striking students, but city officials intervened and demanded that the four suspended students be reinstated.

1936: "STUDENT STRIKE UPSETS TOWN; MAYOR GUARDED"
Alameda High School // Alameda, California

"WE WANT PADEN, HE IS FOR US AND ALWAYS WAS"
"STRIKE STUDENTS STRIKE, LET'S STAND BY HIM"

The Great Depression years of the 1930s were a period of desperation for many Americans. Images of hungry men, women, and children in bread and soup lines dominate popular historical memory. However, the era was also characterized by fierce political clashes, including heated elections and thousands of strikes and labor stoppages all over the country.

In 1935, Alameda, California's new mayor, Hans Roebke, and city manager, Ray Fritz, began instituting sweeping changes to the city's government, replacing several officials, including the entire Social Services Board and the head of the Library Board. On March 3, 1936, the city council also fired popular Superintendent of Schools William Paden.

The next day, several Alameda High School students met with Fritz in an attempt to reverse the decision, but to no avail. The Alameda High student council then voted for a strike, and on March 5, as many as 1,400 students walked out of school and began picketing City Hall. Popular outrage that had been building against Roebke and Fritz over the previous year quickly became support for the students' strike. The local newspaper printed favorable editorials, and the students inspired a "mass meeting...at which citizens went on record for a recall movement against Roebke and two city councilmen." A local hotel even sponsored a dance for the students in order to raise funds for their gas and other "strike supplies."

Worried that the "citizenry was planning to seize" the city government, Mayor Roebke ordered police with shotguns and tear gas bombs to guard his office and threatened to declare an official state of emergency. Alameda County District Attorney Earl Warren warned Roebke, however, that doing so could lead to bloodshed—and that the "parties responsible" for such an escalation would be held accountable. On March 7, Superintendent Paden's firing was ruled void, as he had not violated the terms of his four-year contract. He was reinstated. The students won, and they ended their three-day strike.

Later that year, Mayor Roebke, City Manager Fritz, and other members of the city council were forced to resign after being indicted on a variety of corruption charges, including bribery, petty theft, and perjury. Earl Warren later became Chief Justice of the U.S. Supreme Court, most famously issuing the unanimous majority opinion in the Brown v. Board of Education decision, which outlawed the racial segregation of schools.

1936: THE 1936 STUDENT STRIKE WAVE
St. Helens High School // St. Helens, Oregon
Edison Technical High School // Fresno, California

"DOWN WITH COMPROMISE!"
"POTTS MUST GO!"

The Alameda strike was national news, and within days, the students' victory inspired others to take action, as well.

On March 10, some 379 of the 400 high school students in St. Helens, Oregon left school to protest the firing of their own school superintendent, J.R. Austin. As they took to the streets of St. Helens, students yelled, "Alameda students won, why can't we?"

Some students attempted to enter the office of St. Helens Mayor J.W. Allen, but he refused to open the door. An unsympathetic board member scoffed that the students could "stay out of school 'til next summer for all he cared." But just like in Alameda, the students' protest sparked public interest in recalling local politicians from office. The mounting pressure compelled officials to promise that Superintendent Austin would be retained, and St. Helens students returned to school. When the promise was not kept, they walked out again.

Meanwhile, on March 11, as many as 600 students at Fresno, California's Edison Technical High School left class and marched through the city's streets, citing fifteen grievances and demanding the removal of Principal W.L. Potts. The dispute began with a student complaint that Principal Potts had failed to properly recognize the accomplishments of the school's athletic teams, including the championship-winning basketball team. Potts responded by insulting the students and disparaging their concerns, so student leaders began organizing a strike.

After the students walked out and protested at Courthouse Park, City Superintendent O.S. Hubbard tried to intervene. He addressed the crowd and offered compromise, but he received only boos from the protestors. He then met with student strike leaders, who admitted that they no longer held influence with the student body.

Later that month, after the strike had subsided, Hubbard pressured the student council to pass a resolution banning strikes and protests as a means of redress.

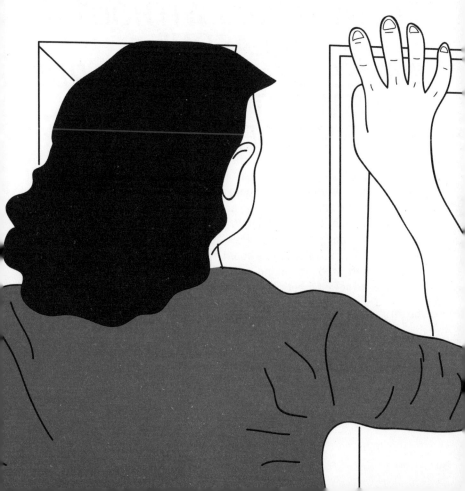

1938: A STRIKE FOR THE STUDENTS' FRIEND
Leyden Township High School // Franklin Park, Illinois

"EVEN CRIMINALS ARE NOT CONDEMNED WITHOUT A REASON"
"INVESTIGATE THE BOARD!"
"WE WANT ALBERT HALL, THE STUDENTS' FRIEND"

In May 1938, Leyden Township High School Principal George Deal recommended to the school board that four employees be fired. The board, led by President Ada Dodge, acquiesced, voting 3-2 not to renew the contracts of athletic director Lynn Watson, teacher Leland Meyer, attorney Richard Locke, and janitor Albert Hall. At least one of the jobs of those fired was to be given to a relative of a board member.

When students found out about the firings, they appointed a committee to seek a meeting with Dodge. She refused.

The next day, 525 students went on strike. Through a spokesperson, they vowed not to return to class until the board reversed its decision. Instead, they protested outside of the school.

The two board members who voted against Principal Deal's proposal contacted the state superintendent to request an investigation into the firings.

1942: INTERNMENT DISSIDENTS
Tule Lake Segregation Center // Tulelake, California

In February 1942, in one of the most shameful moments in modern U.S. history, President Franklin D. Roosevelt issued Executive Order 9066, ordering people of Japanese ancestry to be forcefully removed from their homes and imprisoned in concentration camps in Texas, California, Arizona, Utah, Colorado, Arkansas, and elsewhere. Though they were not charged with crimes and were not given trials, 120,000 Japanese Americans were held in prison camps under armed guard for the duration of World War II. Many lost their homes, jobs, and possessions in the process.

U.S. officials claimed that the concentration camps served the interest of national security. They argued that since the United States was at war with Japan, anyone of Japanese descent, even if born in the U.S., could be a potential spy. Their actions were unconstitutional, and their logic was both paranoid and racist. In fact, the policy was supported by American white supremacists for reasons unrelated to the war.

Adding to the humiliation and injustice of the camps, U.S. officials also forced adults to complete 28 question surveys to determine how "American" they were. Questions ranged from the cultural (questioning their religion, for example) to whether they would join the military and profess total allegiance to the U.S. government. Most inmates cooperated, and many young Japanese-American men joined the U.S. military, even as their families remained in the camps. In fact, Japanese-American troops were among those who liberated Nazi concentration camps.

Other inmates, however, refused to cooperate with the government in any way. Protests and strikes were common, and many prisoners answered "No" on the questionnaires, and rejected military service. Others responded that they would join the war effort when their families were freed.

One of the most disruptive camps was at Tule Lake in California. There, more than 40 percent of respondents answered "No" to the survey's loyalty questions (compared to around 10 percent at other camps). About 35 teenage boys at Tule Lake also protested by refusing to turn in their surveys. They were arrested and taken to a nearby jail at gunpoint. Over the next few months, more than 100 of the camp's inmates were arrested.

Martial law was declared at Tule Lake, and military police took over from civilian authorities, but protests at the overcrowded camp continued. As the war went on, Tule Lake evolved into a maximum-security prison for the camp system—a place for dissidents and "disloyals."

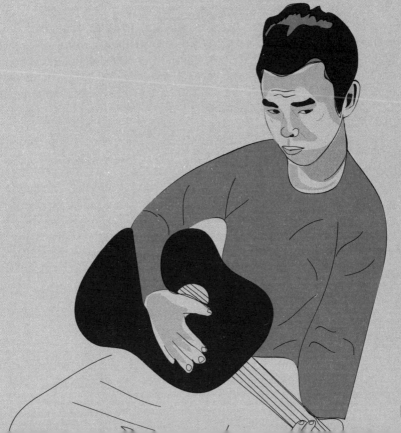

1949: SCOTTSBURG'S NOISY PARADE
Scottsburg High School // Scottsburg, Indiana

"WE WANT BUTLER"
"NO BUTLER? NO SCHOOL!"
"ALL FOR BUTLER"

In the Spring of 1949, the school board of Scottsburg, Indiana announced that the contracts of Principal E.B. Butler and music director Ruby Keel would not be renewed for the following school year. After students and parents presented petitions to board members, they reinstated Keel, but not Butler. Though they had no complaints about his performance, the school board felt that, at sixty, he was simply too old for the job.

On April 6, about half of Scottsburg High School's 280 students went on strike and picketed the school. As the strike expanded into its second day, only eight students arrived for school.

Led by a brass band, drum corps, "and a pretty drum majorette," protesting students marched through the town's business district in a "noisy parade." Some students rode their bikes. Others drove cars (and honked their horns). Many simply walked, carrying signs demanding Butler's return. School board secretary Ivan Gillespie spoke disparagingly of the students, telling reporters, "A good thundershower would break up this whole thing." But as students showed no sign of giving up, the school board was forced to call an emergency community meeting.

At the meeting, student representatives, local business owners, school board members, and parents negotiated an agreement. In exchange for students returning to school the following Monday, the final decision on Butler's future would be decided by Scottsburg High parents in a referendum.

Of the 197 parents who voted, 92 percent backed Butler's return. He signed a new one-year contract within a week of the strike.

The students won.

Their sense of justice was nearly two decades ahead of the curve. In 1967, President Lyndon Johnson signed into law the Age Discrimination in Employment Act (ADEA), forbidding employers from firing (or refusing to hire) workers over forty simply because of their age.

1950: "FORBIDDEN KISS SETS OFF STRIKE AT HIGH SCHOOL"
Bethany High School //
Bethany, Oklahoma

In February 1950, sixteen-year-old Bethany High School student Riddle Riggs gave Charlotte McClain, also sixteen, a playful kiss as he placed a crown on her head during a "Basketball Queen" coronation.

Immediately following the ceremony, two dozen students walked out of school. But their strike was not in opposition to the kiss. Rather, they protested the retaliation that they feared would come from administrators.

Bethany was a small, "blue law" town, meaning it was governed by a series of repressive laws against "dancing, smoking, beer drinking, kissing in public, and women wearing shorts." As one striking student explained, "Bethany High School is a public school, but it is run by strict religious rules. The student council doesn't have enough say-so about school activities."

The striking students attempted to organize an impromptu "protest parade" by driving through the town. However, they were stopped by police because they did not have a permit. The students then asked the mayor for a permit, but he refused, telling them that they could not have a parade because they had put signs on their cars "which said students at the high school did not have enough freedom."

1950: "30,000 STUDENTS RIOT ON TEACHER PAY ISSUE"
New York, New York

"NO SCHOOL THIS WEEK, YOU'RE RESPONSIBLE O'DWYER"

After being denied a cost of living raise in April 1950, New York City schoolteachers announced that they would no longer volunteer for unpaid extra-curricular activities, such as chaperoning at dances and sporting events. On Tuesday, April 25, several hundred students from Brooklyn Technical High School and New Utrecht High School responded by walking out of class and marching to City Hall. By noon, however, the students had dispersed with little fanfare.

But, the next day, as many as 10,000 students walked out of class. Police estimated that 9,000 paraded in front of their Brooklyn schools, while 1,000 marched on City Hall ("most of them girls," according to one news report). Several hundred students from Roosevelt High in the Bronx pushed past police in order to reach the office of Mayor William O'Dwyer, but he was not there.

By Thursday, the student strike reached numbers as high as 30,000, in groups of hundreds and thousands in parks and streets all over the city. Several thousand students flooded across the Williamsburg and Manhattan Bridges from Brooklyn. Yelling "More pay for our teachers!" large groups marched on City Hall in hopes of pressuring Mayor O'Dwyer to grant the raises. Said one of the protesting teens, "Mayor O'Dwyer gave himself a fat raise, and he takes plenty of vacations. But he doesn't seem to worry about the teachers who aren't even paid for their extra hours of work." Another explained, "This is the least we can do to help both ourselves and our teachers."

Mayor O'Dwyer, however, refused to meet with them, while Superintendent of Schools William Jansen blamed "subversive groups" for the protests. The mayor ordered a massive police presence to defend City Hall and his home—reportedly "100 patrolmen and 25 mounted men [on horses]." Meanwhile, the FBI joined the police effort, passing along an anonymous tip that students planned to lure police away with a diversion, so that a separate student group could "take the hall." The protests grew large and heated, leading to arrests and other clashes with police. Some of the students even overturned a parked car.

The story quickly became national news, with headlines like "20,000 Boro Students Strike, Stage March on City Hall," "FBI Joins Cops Against N.Y. Students," and "30,000 Students Riot on Teacher Pay Issue."

Following threats from the Mayor and Superintendent, the protests died down by the end of the week. In the Fall of 1951, teachers and city officials reached a compromise, and extra-curricular activities resumed.

1951: DAVIS V. PRINCE EDWARD COUNTY
Farmville High School // Farmville, Virginia

"This is your moment. *Seize it!*"

In 1954, the U.S. Supreme Court ruled unanimously in Brown v. Board of Education of Topeka, Kansas that laws requiring racially segregated public education violated the 14th Amendment rights of students. The case was named for the lawsuit filed by thirteen African-American parents in Kansas, but it actually combined five similar cases. The others had challenged segregation in Delaware, South Carolina, Virginia, and Washington, D.C.

The Virginia case, Davis v. County School Board of Prince Edward County, originated with a two-week student strike at Robert Russa Moton High School in Farmville, Virginia.

In stark contrast to facilities for white students at Farmville High, Moton High students had neither a gym nor a cafeteria, and the school district responded to overcrowding at the school by building tarpaper shacks. Fed up, in April 1951, sixteen-year-old Barbara Rose Johns, among others, organized 450 students to walk out and demand a new school. Said Johns, "There wasn't any fear. I just thought, 'This is your moment. Seize it!'" After a mass community meeting at Farmville's First Baptist Church, students agreed to shift their demand from a new school to an end to segregation. Led by attorneys Spottswood Robinson, Oliver Hill, and Robert Carter, the NAACP launched Davis v. Prince Edward County on behalf of 117 Moton High students (including 9th grader Dorothy Davis, for whom it was named).

Local white officials scrambled to build a brand new Moton High School, so that they could tell the courts that "separate but equal" facilities existed. The ploy paid off, and Virginia's segregation laws were upheld until the Brown case.

After the Supreme Court made its Brown ruling, officials in states like Texas, Arkansas, Florida, and Alabama launched a campaign called Massive Resistance, opposing desegregation however they could. In Virginia, the Farmville school board, rather than cooperate with Brown, opted to close all of its public schools in 1959, and they remained closed until 1964. In the meantime, the town's white students attended all-white private schools, where they were taught by the same white teachers that they would have had at Farmville High.

Winning the Brown case changed U.S. law. Enforcing that law, however, was another fight.

1956: BRICK WALLS AND PICKET LINES
M.C. Napier High School // Hazard, Kentucky

In April 1956, the Perry County school board announced that Napier High School Principal Walter Martin, Jr. "might not be rehired" for the following year.

In response, 750 Napier High students went on strike for a week. According to newspaper reports, the students "piled bricks in front of entrances and set up picket lines to keep the classrooms empty."

The strike finally ended when Principal Martin himself appealed to twenty members of the student council to develop an alternative plan of protest. After meeting with Martin, the students signed a pledge to end their walkout and announced that they would "seek some other means" to challenge the school board. Meanwhile, the student council asked "all students who had reached Kentucky's legal voting age of eighteen" to support "our cause" by voting out the school board.

"WE DEMAND A FAIR TRIAL"
"WE DEMAND JUSTICE IN HUBBARD HI"

In March 1957, twelve students at Hubbard High School presented Superintendent Kenneth St. John with a list of grievances about what students called "objectionable rules." A week later, after a scuffle with a teacher, one of the students, William Benjamin, was expelled.

Though the school board claimed that the two incidents were unrelated and that William Benjamin's expulsion was not a case of retaliation, many disagreed.

Led by William Benjamin's mother, between ten and twenty mothers picketed the school. Their signs read, "WE DEMAND A FAIR TRIAL," "WHY ARE SOME STUDENTS MORE PRIVILEGED," and "WE DEMAND JUSTICE IN HUBBARD HI."

As students arrived to school on April 2, the mothers asked them, "Are you against Benjamin?" Roughly 400 students, about half of the student body, responded that they were not—and joined the mothers' protest.

1957: THE LITTLE ROCK 9
Little Rock Central High School //
Little Rock, Arkansas

The 1954 Brown v. Board of Education Supreme Court decision was one of many legal victories for civil rights activists. In the Brown case, the court ruled that racially segregated schools were unconstitutional. However, winning the case did not automatically desegregate schools. That task was left to students themselves.

In the Fall of 1957, nine African-American teens enrolled at Little Rock Central High School. When they attempted to enter the school on the first day of classes, however, they were greeted by an angry mob of white racists and barred from entry, at gunpoint, by the Arkansas National Guard, on the order of Governor Orval Faubus.

After an intervention by U.S. President Dwight Eisenhower, Faubus recalled the National Guard, but left the students and local police to contend with (pro-Faubus) segregationist protestors—who threatened to murder the students and had already brutally attacked black journalists. The white supremacists carried signs with slogans like:

"RACE MIXING IS COMMUNISM," "SAVE OUR CHRISTIAN AMERICA," and "SAVE OUR CONSTITUTION— FOLLOW FAUBUS."

Despite constant threats and incidents of violence, the defiant "Little Rock 9" returned to the school, and, at the request of the mayor, President Eisenhower sent soldiers from the Army's 101st Airborne Division (complete with machine guns, helicopters, and fixed bayonets) to escort them to class. That year, soldiers accompanied each of the nine students, but they were still subjected to harassment and attacks from their white classmates.

At the end of that year, Ernest Green became the first African-American graduate of Little Rock Central High School. But the struggle did not end there. As part of Southern white supremacists' agreement to resist racial equality by any means at their disposal, Governor Faubus cancelled the 1958 school year altogether.

1960: **THE LUNCH COUNTER SIT-IN CAMPAIGN**
Dudley High School //
Greensboro, North Carolina

On February 1, 1960, four African-American students from North Carolina A&T University sat down at the "whites only" section of a lunch counter at Woolworth department store in Greensboro, North Carolina. They ordered coffee, but they were denied service.

They left when the store closed, but they returned the next day and again sat down. For the rest of the week, they returned again and again, with ever-larger crowds of supporters, including students from nearby Dudley High School. Large groups of white supremacists, including members of the Ku Klux Klan, also began arriving to heckle, harass, and attack the young civil rights activists. On February 6, someone called in a bomb threat to Woolworth, so the protestors moved to nearby S.H. Kress—another "five and dime" store. Within weeks, the lunch counter "sit-ins," largely led by college and high school students, had spread to cities all over the American South in states including South Carolina, Florida, Tennessee, and Virginia. Solidarity pickets also targeted Woolworth stores in the North.

On February 11, 26 high school students in High Point, North Carolina organized a sit-in at their local Woolworth store. It was one of the few such demonstrations orchestrated entirely by high school students. By the end of March, there were ongoing sit-ins in more than 55 cities in thirteen states, but business leaders still refused to de-segregate their stores. So, the sit-ins continued.

On April 1, fifteen students from Burke High School in Charleston, South Carolina, were arrested during sit-ins that targeted the city's Kress, Woolworth, and W.T. Grant department stores. Back in Greensboro, college let out in June, and Dudley High students took over the movement, expanding it to Meyer's and Walgreen's stores.

In July, they won. Five months of disrupting business and attracting negative publicity had finally become more persuasive than the support of white supremacists, and Woolworth and Kress store officials announced that they would finally end their racist seating policies.

1963: FREEDOM DAY
Chicago, Illinois

"SUPPORT OUR BOYCOTT"
"GIVE OUR CHILDREN A CHANCE"
"PUT WILLIS OUT— WITHOUT A DOUBT!!"
"DOWN WITH BEN. AMEN."

The year 1963 was a significant one for anti-racist actions. In April and May, thousands of students in Birmingham, Alabama participated in a campaign to end racial discrimination in employment and social life. After Birmingham's jails were filled beyond capacity with arrested demonstrators, City Commissioner Eugene "Bull" Connor turned police attack dogs and high-pressure fire hoses on activists (including children), setting up some of the most iconic and disturbing photographs of the period. Nearly 1,000 young people were arrested.

That August, hundreds of thousands of people participated in the "March on Washington" to demand an end to segregation and "jobs for all." At a massive protest on the National Mall, Martin Luther King, Jr., gave his iconic "I Have a Dream" speech.

Two months later, an alliance of civil rights groups in Chicago organized "Freedom Day" to protest overcrowding and segregation in their city's schools and, more specifically, the policies of Superintendent Benjamin C. Willis. On October 22, roughly 150,000 students from the city's

550 schools—many of them high school students—engaged in a one-day boycott of public schools. Schools in predominantly black neighborhoods were "nearly emptied." The day then culminated with perhaps 10,000 chanting, singing protestors (white and black) marching around both City Hall and the Board of Education office—and "jamming" rush hour traffic in the loop. Their signs called for an end to racism and harshly criticized Willis.

Addressing the crowd, the head of the Chicago chapter of the NAACP cried, "The time for victory is here in Chicago, as well as in Birmingham. The time is now for [ousting] Ben Willis in Chicago as well as Governor [George] Wallace in Alabama!"

1968: THE EAST L.A. BLOWOUTS
Los Angeles, California

"VIVA LA CAUSA!"
"VIVA LA RAZA!"
"CHICANO POWER!"

In the late 1960s, Anglo-centric textbooks, poor funding for schools, and the racist assumptions of teachers and administrators combined to create a no-win educational system for Mexican-American youth in the American Southwest. Dropout rates hovered around 50 percent, and those who graduated did not fare much better—averaging an eighth grade reading level and having been largely steered toward vocational training instead of college preparation.

To protest this crisis, in March 1968, 15,000 to 20,000 Mexican-American students marched out of class at Lincoln, Roosevelt, Belmont, Venice, and Jefferson High Schools in East Los Angeles. The walkouts, which students called "blowouts," were supported by a variety of community organizers, activists from area universities, and some teachers. At some schools, attempts to block the students led to clashes with police.

The students' 39 demands to the school district included bilingual and bicultural education, textbooks and curriculum "revised to show Mexican contributions to society" and the "injustices they have suffered," the re-naming of schools to honor "Mexican heroes" and "establish community identity," the inclusion of Mexican food in school cafeteria menus, the improvement of school libraries, and an end to cultural prejudice by teachers and administrators. The students also demanded student-run student union spaces and free speech areas, the right to invite political speakers, and an end to corporal punishment (spanking and hitting).

But although members of the school board agreed in principle with "99 percent of the demands," they claimed that budget limitations prevented them from taking action. Instead, police arrested thirteen of the adults who had supported the blowouts and charged them with conspiracy to disturb the peace. Each faced 66 years in prison if convicted. An ACLU legal defense, protests at the police station and courthouse, and a weeklong sit-in at the school board office eventually forced their release—and the re-instatement of teachers who had been suspended for their involvement.

In the years that followed, there were similar student walkouts in Tucson, Arizona as well as Crystal City, Kingsville, and Robstown, Texas, among other places. The movement also expanded its focus to include opposition to the Vietnam War through the Chicano Moratorium movement.

1968: **THE MINNEAPOLIS SCHOOL BOARD PICKET**
Roosevelt High School // Minneapolis, Minnesota

"WE WANT SHORTS!" "COME OUT OF THE STONE AGE, CULOTTES ARE NOW" "WE LIKE HAIRY LEGS" "TIMES ARE CHANGING, WHAT ABOUT OUR DRESS CODE?"

In May 1968, the Minneapolis School Board overturned proposed changes to Roosevelt High School's dress code, which would have allowed boys to wear "Bermuda shorts" on hot days and girls to wear "slacks" on cold days. According to Superintendent Nathaniel Ober, the school district's citywide ban on shorts and slacks trumped the wishes of Roosevelt High.

In response, more than 300 Roosevelt students picketed outside of the school board's meeting, carrying signs reading, "WE LIKE HAIRY LEGS", "WE WANT SHORTS!" and "KNOBBY KNEES ARE IN."

Receiving no support from the school board, students decided to escalate their tactics. After the board meeting, the Roosevelt High School student council president announced that on the following Friday, boys at the school would deliberately break the rules—by wearing shorts!

"OPEN THE WALLETS, OPEN THE SCHOOLS" "DON'T LOCK US OUT!" "KIDS CAN'T, YOU CAN. SUPPORT PUBLIC EDUCATION"

Between 1962 and 1968, voters in Youngstown, Ohio rejected six different attempts to raise taxes for public schools. Despite borrowing 1.5 million dollars from banks in August 1968, the school district had just 6 thousand dollars with which to meet its 1 million dollar December pay roll. Unable to legally borrow additional funds until January, school officials had to shut down all 45 of Youngstown's schools. When the city's 27,000 students went home for Thanksgiving break, they were told to stay home until the new year.

On Monday, December 2, when classes should have resumed, 50 students from Rayen High School marched through downtown Youngstown. They chanted, "Education, not vacation!" and carried signs, reading, "OPEN THE WALLETS, OPEN THE SCHOOLS" and "DON'T LOCK US OUT!" A photo of the marching students ran in newspapers all over the country.

The following May, facing the possibility that the next school year might not happen at all, Youngstown voters finally approved education funding.

1969: TINKER V. DES MOINES
North High School // Des Moines, Iowa

During the 1960s era, high school students in the United States participated in a variety of social movements, many of which demanded the rights of marginalized groups, including African Americans, women, Mexican Americans, American Indians, Asian Americans, and migrant workers, among others. However, exactly which legal rights applied to the teenagers themselves was an open question.

In December 1965, North High School students John Tinker (age fifteen) and Christopher Eckhardt (age sixteen), as well as John's younger siblings Mary Beth (age thirteen), Hope (age eleven), and Paul (age eight) wore black armbands to their Des Moines, Iowa schools to protest the Vietnam War. Their school principals found out about the plan in advance and quickly instituted a rule banning armbands. When they arrived at school in violation of the new policy, John, Christopher, and Mary Beth were suspended. After winter break, they returned without the bands (they had planned all along to end their demonstration on January 1), but they wore black in protest for the remainder of the year.

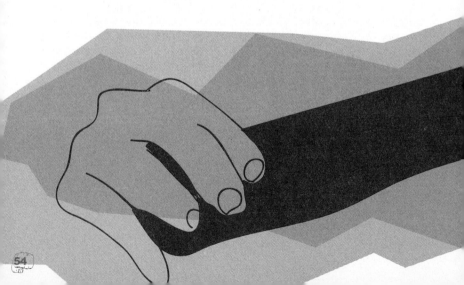

Represented by the American Civil Liberties Union (ACLU), the students challenged the school district's ban, but the Tinker v. Des Moines Independent Community School District case was upheld at every level, until it reached the U.S. Supreme Court in 1969.

In Tinker v. Des Moines, the Supreme Court ruled that while children were not entitled to full First Amendment rights, their freedom of speech also did not entirely disappear when on school grounds. The justices concluded that public school students had a right to express themselves, as long as that expression did not "materially and substantially" disrupt the school's operations. In other words, passive protest (like the armbands) was protected by students' First Amendment rights, and the Des Moines schools' ban was unconstitutional.

The students won, and the "Tinker test" is often still applied when assessing students' freedom of expression.

1969: A PROTEST ON THE NEW YORK CAPITOL LAWN
New York State Legislature // Albany, New York

"USE TAXES TO BUILD, NOT IN VIETNAM TO BURN"
"TAX THE ROCKEFELLERS, NOT THE POOR FELLOWS"

In 1969, mirroring a nationwide trend for public education budgets, New York Governor Nelson Rockefeller announced his intention to cut millions of dollars of funding from the seventeen schools in the City University of New York (CUNY) system.

On March 18, as many as 10,000 high school and college students from New York City traveled to Albany to protest their state legislature. The students—black, white, and Puerto Rican—arrived on more than 230 chartered buses. Their demands ranged from a general opposition to the state's education cuts to a specific focus on maintaining funding for SEEK, a program for low-income college students.

Many of the students entered the state assembly building carrying protest signs but remaining orderly. When told to remove their signs, however, students began some "mild taunting" of their representatives. As Assemblyman Neil Kelleher called for order, another official called for him to "throw those animals out." In response, one of the students yelled, "Throw out the legislators." Kelleher called for the state police, but when they arrived, they found the students sitting quietly.

Meanwhile outside, several Democrats, the minority in both New York houses, greeted student protestors and promised to do their best to fight the cuts. As they gave their statements, however, several students interrupted what they viewed as "insincere oratory." Some began chanting,

"What about SEEK? What about SEEK?"

Others called for protestors to escalate their actions and occupy a government building.

Ultimately, the students returned to New York City without any guarantees from state legislators. They announced that the following week, they would picket New York City Hall, another source of sweeping education cuts.

1969: A FUNERAL FOR EDUCATION
Waukegan Township High School //
Waukegan, Illinois

In yet another blow to public education, voters in Waukegan, Illinois rejected a referendum to raise taxes for schools in the Fall of 1969. School district administrators announced in response that the resulting budget cuts would likely force them to eliminate extra-curricular activities.

On the evening of October 28, more than 500 Waukegan Township High School students marched ten blocks from their school to the Lake County Court House, where they held a candlelight vigil. They carried with them a mock casket, which they said contained "the remains" of public education.

A student spokesperson told journalists that they were planning additional protests to bring attention to the needs of students.

1970: JEFFERS V. YUBA CITY UNIFIED SCHOOL DISTRICT
Yuba City Union High School // Yuba City, California

In February 1970, administrators at Yuba City Union High School implemented new rules for boys' haircuts. They prohibited beards and moustaches, required sideburns to stop at the ear lobe, and banned hair that covered ears, shirt collars, or eyes. Long hair was a sign of the hippie counterculture, whose love of rock 'n roll (and opposition to the Vietnam War) marked a clear generational divide. According to Principal John Stremple, there was "a detrimental relationship between long hair and the so-called hippie culture." Stremple also said that the students who used and sold drugs were those "most involved in the long hair culture."

At the beginning of the school year, the student council passed a resolution against the new rules, and a poll found that 83.7 percent of students opposed the hair restrictions. A more broadly worded survey of parents, however, revealed support for the rules by a margin of 1,078 to 194. The school's Board of Trustees upheld the new policy over the protests of the student council.

The next month, Yuba City High students Merle Jeffers, Jr. (age sixteen) and Stephen Smith (age seventeen) were suspended for their long hair. In response, they filed a lawsuit against the school, claiming that the policy violated their first and fourteenth Amendment rights. According to their attorney, the boys' long hair was a statement that they wanted to "reject the hairstyles of another generation—the generation of their parents." In court, P.E. teachers testified that long hair covering boys' eyes was dangerous, while a member of the school board argued that if long hair were allowed, "they would see a breakdown in the general disciplinary structure."

Ultimately, Judge Philip Wilkins ruled against the students. Wilkins noted that freedom of speech and freedom of expression were not the same, and that the Tinker v. Des Moines ruling specifically made exceptions for hairstyle and dress code. However, most disturbingly, the judge noted that Yuba City administrators had proven that long hair was in fact disruptive to

the school, because boys with long hair were often physically attacked by other students.

In other words, "long hairs" could be forced to cut their hair because bullies wanted them to.

1970: EARTH DAY
Brookfield High School // Brookfield, Connecticut

On April 22, 1970, over 20 million Americans participated in the first Earth Day. There were protests and other activities in towns and cities all over the country. In Connecticut, April 22 was "a day for the ceremonial burying of automobile engines, drafting citizens to ride garbage trucks, teach-ins, and bicycle parades," according to one newspaper account.

Since Earth Day fell during their Spring Break, students at Brookfield High School opted to recognize the event during the week prior. Students were asked to "walk, horseback ride, or pedal bikes to school—but not come by air-polluting car." As they arrived at school, a long procession of students on bikes and on foot "clogged Longmeadow Hill Road," effectively halting traffic. The Brookfield High student council also called for a "community-wide boycott of throw-away bottles."

At nearby New Milford High School, students collected litter from all over town and piled it in the common space outside of their school. They then used the garbage as a prop in a daylong teach-in and organized a bicycle parade around the school.

Yet another area school, Danbury High, hosted an ecology-themed science fair that featured student "displays and posters" on "air and water pollution, garbage disposal, insecticides and related matters." Many other grade schools, high schools, colleges, and community groups in the area also hosted teach-ins and panel discussions, movie screenings, litter clean-ups, parades, and other environment-themed programs.

Within months of Earth Day, the U.S. government established the Environmental Protection Agency (EPA), and over the next few years, Congress also expanded the Clean Air Act and passed both the Safe Drinking Water Act and the Endangered Species Act.

1972: TITLE IX
United States Congress //
Washington, DC

"No person in the United States shall, on the basis of sex, be excluded from participation in, be denied benefits of, or be subjected to discrimination under any education program or activity receiving Federal financial assistance."

The Women's Liberation Movement of the 1960s and 1970s was massive, diverse, and successful. Feminist activists dramatically changed the social rights of American women, compelled the passage of a series of laws (for example, outlawing sexual harassment), and founded nearly 1,000 rape crisis centers across the country. The movement also came very close to forcing the passage of an amendment to the U.S. Constitution that would have outlawed sexual discrimination.

One of the women's movement's clearest victories was the passage of Title IX (nine). As part of Congress' Education Amendments of 1972, Title IX effectively banned sexist discrimination in public schools. Like other legal changes during the period, though, compelling the federal government to actually implement the law took years of agitation by activists.

Most famously, Title IX led to the funding of girls' and women's athletics in high schools and colleges. Indeed, before the law passed, fewer than 300,000 American girls participated in high school athletics. By 2010, more than 3.2 million did.

However, Title IX has also had major impacts on girls' and women's educational opportunities. It continues to help women (and men) combat sexual harassment and bullying, and it provides opportunities for pregnant and parenting teens to continue their education. In recent years, activists have used Title IX to challenge weak policies against rape and sexual assault at American universities.

Contrary to popular myths, Title IX does not implement a quota system and has not hampered boys' participation in sports, which has also grown steadily in the period since the bill's passage.

1978: THE ORACLE STAFF STRIKE
Dwight Morrow High School //
Englewood, New Jersey

"We'll hold fast."

In September 1978, Dwight Morrow High School Principal Charles Hall announced that English and Journalism teacher Kathy Echave was being replaced as adviser to the student newspaper, the *Oracle*. Echave had served as faculty adviser to the award-winning paper for seven years.

The same month, when student editor Melanie Peters attempted to pick up the paper's September proofs, she was shocked to find that they had already been taken. According to the print shop, they were picked up by a mysterious "middle-aged man" who claimed to have permission from school authorities. That man turned out to be Principal Hall.

Principal Hall claimed that he picked up the proofs in order to deliver them to the new adviser, but students suspected him of trying to censor their paper. Hall and the *Oracle* had a history of conflict, and he had steadily cut its budget in years prior. Hall also claimed that Echave was only being replaced because she had failed to meet the application renewal deadline, which he had moved up three months from its usual date. He could not, however, explain why his new appointee had not applied for the job.

According to Echave, the administrators' excuse was "a ploy." She explained, "I've been replaced simply because of my attitude toward the newspaper. I let the students express their opinion and write the truth, but the administration wanted what it called 'more positive' stories. They wanted a public relations tool."

In response to the two incidents, the staff at the *Oracle* went on strike. Students contacted the ACLU, while Echave contacted the teachers' union. Editor Melanie Peters vowed, "We're still on strike, and we'll hold fast until we get our adviser back."

Two weeks later, teachers and students presented their case to the city school board, along with a petition of support signed by 60 teachers.

The students won. Kathy Echave was reinstated as advisor to the Oracle.

1980: THE FIRST LEGAL DANCE IN ELMORE CITY
Elmore City High School // Elmore City, Oklahoma

For more than 80 years, public dancing was outlawed in the small town of Elmore City, Oklahoma. But in 1980, high school students petitioned the school board to lift the ban so that they could host a prom. The clash that ensued became a national news story and inspired the popular 1984 film Footloose, starring Kevin Bacon.

Elmore City's 653 residents were split on the dancing issue. Conservative locals warned that the dance would lead to a spike in teen pregnancy, because "when boys and girls breathe in each other's ears, that's the next step." A minister from a nearby town explained, "If you have a dance, somebody will crash it and they'll be looking for only two things—women and booze. When boys and girls hold each other, they get sexually aroused. You can believe what you want, but one thing leads to another."

The movie plot of Footloose relied on the influence of an outsider from a big city (a transfer student played by Bacon), but the real-life agitation came from within Elmore City itself. The demand was simple. As class president Rex Kennedy told the board, "We would like to have a few nice memories."

Their campaign paid off, and the board voted 3-2 to allow the dance. Students responded by organizing a series of benefits and raised 2 thousand dollars—enough for a dinner and decorations to transform their school cafeteria. The prom's theme was Led Zeppelin's "Stairway to Heaven," and student organizers also set up a game room for those who wanted a break from the dance floor.

Although the students did not need Kevin Bacon to challenge the board, they could have used his dancing lessons! As one prom date lamented, "I sure wish they'd play more slow songs. I can't do the fast stuff yet."

1980: **THE SEATTLE SCHOOL DISTRICT PICKET**
Abraham Lincoln High School //
Seattle, Washington

"SAVE LINCOLN"
"WE LOVE LINCOLN, KEEP IT OPEN!"

In 1980, Seattle Public Schools announced that Abraham Lincoln High School, established in 1907, would close the following Spring, amid declining enrollment. In November, Lincoln High students picketed at the school district headquarters wearing paper protest hats and carrying "SAVE LINCOLN" signs. But they were unable to sway administrators.

Lincoln closed in 1981, and on its last day, students, faculty, and alumni gathered on the school's front steps to sing the school song, say goodbye, and close the book on a rich and complex history.

In the 1940s, Lincoln's Japanese-American students, including the editor of the student newspaper, had been among those forced into internment camps.

In 1953, the school hired English teacher Warren Littlejohn, the first African-American teacher at any Seattle public high school.

In 1973, Lincoln High School hired Principal Roberta Byrd Barr, who was both the first African-American principal and the first female principal of a Seattle public high school. Barr, a life-long civil rights activist, actress, and educator, had organized one of several "Freedom Schools" during a citywide student boycott in 1966. During that campaign, as many as 4,000 students skipped school to protest racial segregation.

Though Lincoln High students moved elsewhere after 1981, the building remained intact, and it was used as a temporary home for several area schools, including Ballard High, Roosevelt High, and Garfield High, during their own buildings' renovations.

Then, in 2012, the Seattle School Board announced an ambitious plan for renovating and expanding area schools, and Seattle voters approved the funds a few months later. Their plan included modernizing and re-opening Lincoln High in 2019.

1981: "ABSTINENCE-ONLY" EDUCATION
United States Congress // Washington, DC

In 1981, President Ronald Reagan signed into law the Adolescent Family Life Act (AFLA), which provided funding for youth education programs to promote sexual abstinence. The law's clear religious influence led to a challenge in the U.S. Supreme Court case Bowen v. Kendrick, but the law was upheld.

In 1996, as part of his assault on poverty programs, President Bill Clinton expanded "abstinence-only" funding from a few million dollars per year to around 50 million dollars per year. President George W. Bush then more than tripled funding to roughly 170 million dollars annually, until it was scaled back to around 50 million dollars per year by President Barack Obama.

In all, more than 1.5 billion federal tax dollars have been spent to promote heterosexist, Christian propaganda that "sex should be confined to married couples," to quote two of its architects. The promise of these funds has also been used to compel states to abandon alternatives (by providing matching funds only to states that agreed to stick to the abstinence-only curriculum).

Abstinence-only programs have been shown to include factually inaccurate information about pregnancy, birth control, sexually transmitted infections, and abortion.

However, according to a 2007 study by the U.S. Department of Health and Human Services, the programs have not had a statistically significant impact on the sexual behavior of American youth.

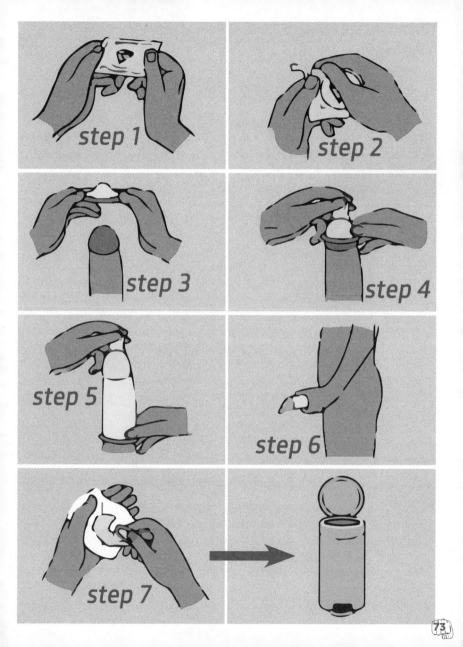

step 1

step 2

step 3

step 4

step 5

step 6

step 7

1986: 924 GILMAN STREET
Berkeley, California

"NO RACISM, NO SEXISM, NO HOMOPHOBIA, NO ALCOHOL, NO DRUGS, NO FIGHTING"

In 1986, several young people, with assistance and funding from the punk rock magazine *MaximumRocknRoll*, founded an all ages, volunteer-run punk venue called 924 Gilman Street. The tasks at the club—from running the sound system, to booking the bands, to providing security and cleaning up—were performed by volunteers, primarily teenagers, and the venue's rules and policies were decided democratically, by consensus, at monthly meetings.

Since the space was run by and for young people, the club instituted only the most basic and necessary rules: no drugs or alcohol allowed (in order to make the venue open to youth of all ages), no racism, sexism, homophobia, or fighting allowed (in order to make the venue a safe space for everyone), and the venue had to be democratically run by all attendees (in order to make entire audiences accountable for enforcing the other rules).

Over its nearly 30 years of existence, 924 Gilman Street has provided thousands of teens a place to hang out and experience live music. More importantly, it has also been a space for young people to shape their world by confronting sexist behavior, breaking up fights, and taking on other responsibilities at the club.

Thousands of bands have also played at Gilman, including well known locals like Green Day, Operation Ivy, Samiam, Neurosis, Jawbreaker, and less famous groups like Kamala and Karnivores and Spitboy. But in the egalitarian spirit of punk rock, 924 Gilman remains a place for community, not for hero-worship. The divide between bands and the audience remains minimal, as most audience members were themselves involved in the scene—in bands of their own, as volunteers at the club, or as writers of zines.

Dozens of similar youth-run, all-ages punk rock clubs have been established in cities all over the U.S. (and around the world), including 1919 Hemphill in Fort Worth, Texas, ABC No Rio in New York City, and the Vera Project in Seattle, Washington.

1990: THE STUDENTS FOR A BETTER SOCIETY RECYCLING PROGRAM
Palmetto High School // Palmetto, Florida

Many U.S. high schools have recycling programs that rely on the efforts of student activists. In California, students coordinate recycling programs and recycling drives at Patrick Henry High School in San Diego and Notre Dame High School in Sherman Oaks, among other places

In some areas, recycling programs were initiated by administrators or city officials, but in many, these programs did not exist until students and teachers started them.

In the Spring of 1990, members of Students for a Better Society at Palmetto High School in Florida launched a recycling program for paper. SBS members placed boxes next to garbage cans in classrooms and collected the paper each Thursday morning.

Two years later, students at Oxford Hills High School in South Paris, Maine began a recycling program of their own. Under the guidance of their English teacher, Brewster Burns, students launched an environmental research project with the aim of educating themselves and their fellow students so that they could expand their school's recycling program.

In 1996, Woonsocket High School in Rhode Island started a recycling program that is still maintained by students for class credit.

In 2001, the Recycling Club at Tuscaloosa County High School in Northport, Alabama (with help from their city council) won a 10 thousand dollar state grant for recycling. They used it to buy a portable recycling trailer for their school as well as recycling bins for all of the classrooms.

In 2008, a student at Rogers High School in Newport, Rhode Island launched a recycling program as a senior project, and it was continued by a student group called the "Green Team."

Taking these efforts one step further, many high schools have also launched composting programs for their food scraps, including Crawford High School in San Diego, Greenfield High School in Greenfield, Massachusetts, and Magnificat High School in Cleveland, Ohio.

1995: BARCIK, KASTEN, ET AL. V. TIGARD-TUALATIN SCHOOL DISTRICT
Tigard High School // Tigard, Oregon

In December 1991, Tigard High School senior Scott Barcik was caught circulating flyers to recruit contributors for *Low-Spots*, an unauthorized, underground student newspaper (and an alternative to the official student paper, *Hi-Spots*). The school's vice principal warned Barcik that he and his friends would be punished if they published the paper without official approval.

After winter break, Barcik and the *Low-Spots* team defied the administration by distributing copies of their irreverent, critical, and mildly profane paper. They were called to the principal's office and threatened with suspension.

In response to the banning of Low-Spots, the editors of its award-winning (and officially sanctioned) counterpart decided to review the publication and write an editorial about the free speech implications of the school's ban. But when the principal heard about the editorial, he contacted the superintendent and the school board, who then demanded its removal from the paper. The *Hi-Spots* editors, including Shannon Kasten, withdrew the editorial, but they printed in its place, in red ink,

"CENSORED BY: MARK KUBIACZYK, RUSS JOKI, AL DAVIDIAN, TIGARD-TUALATIN SCHOOL BOARD."

The next week, the Tigard-Tualatin school board approved extensive new guidelines for student publications, now requiring prior approval by administrators, and also offered a series of reasons why publications could be censored or rejected.

With the help of the ACLU, Barcik, Kasten, and others sued the principal and the school district, and the case eventually reached the Oregon Supreme Court. The court ruled that since the students (having since graduated) were no longer impacted, they could not challenge the continuing policy. However, the court also found that the school had, in fact, violated the students' free speech rights. Neither the distribution of *Low-Spots* or the editorial in *Hi-Spots* could be justified as disturbing the educational process.

The students won, even if only in principle.

LOW SPOTS

CENSORED BY: MARK KUBIACZYK, RUSS JOKI, AL DAVIDIAN, TIGARD-TUALATIN SCHOOL BOARD.

1999: THE PORT CHARLOTTE 14
Port Charlotte High School // Port Charlotte, Florida

In March 1999, the Charlotte County Public School Board announced a plan to shorten their school day, in order to save nearly 1 million dollars and eliminate twenty-two teaching positions. Though the board scheduled its meeting for 9:30 a.m. on a school day, several students from area schools attended and urged the board not to make the change.

Hours later, despite a threatening warning from Principal Charles Patteson over the school's intercom system, about 100 Port Charlotte High School students walked out of class and gathered in the school's courtyard to protest the cuts.

One graduating senior, despite being unaffected by the change, explained that she wanted to do her part to maintain the academic integrity of the school. "I want this school to be good because this school has been good to me," she said.

Repeated threats convinced most of the protesting students to return to class, but fourteen refused and began walking away from the school, toward the district's administration building. Said one student, "We were walking calmly. We weren't causing a riot." Nonetheless, administrators and the campus police officer stopped them from leaving and ordered them to report to the office for a ten-day suspension. The irony of kicking them out of school for opposing cuts to education was not lost on the students or their parents.

When asked why a peaceful demonstration carried the same stiff penalty as bringing a weapon or drugs to school, Principal Patteson replied, "It's in there with those other things because it's just that serious."

Parents disagreed. Under pressure, Patteson reduced the suspensions from ten days to four. He resigned the following year.

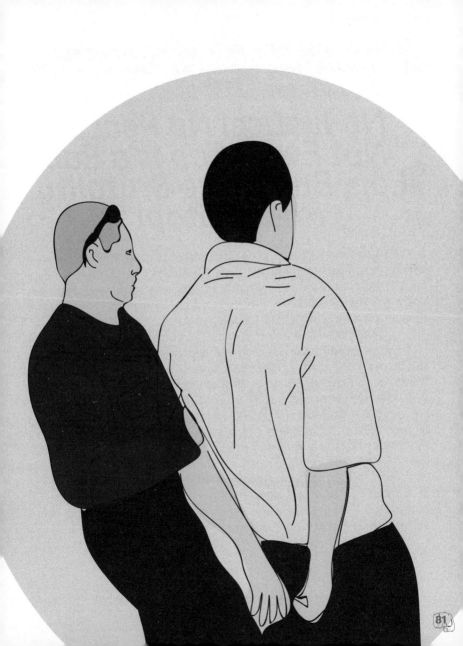

81

2000: JUSTICE FOR AMADOU DIALLO
Stuyvesant High School // New York, New York

"No Justice! No Peace!"
"Not Every Cop Is a Bad Cop, But Police Brutality Has to Stop!"

In 1999, four New York City police officers shot to death Amadou Diallo, a twenty-three-year-old immigrant from the African country Guinea. Police fired 41 shots at Diallo, hitting him a total of nineteen times. Diallo was unarmed. The four officers were indicted on charges of second-degree murder, but were acquitted the following year.

In response to the verdict, two hundred students from Stuyvesant High School walked out of class and marched "noisily but peacefully" across the Brooklyn Bridge to a protest rally against police violence. There they were joined by several hundred other students from La Guardia High School, Edward R. Murrow High School, the Beacon School, and Wingate High School.

Stuyvesant senior Matt Kelly told the New York Times, "We want to let people know that as the next generation, we will not stand for the police misconduct that has become systematic in New York recently."

Even student organizers were surprised by the high turnout, but as sophomore Ben Abelson remarked, "There's a lot of different groups at Stuyvesant who don't get along: the ravers, the preps, the freaks. We all have different interests, but this shows that if we all care enough about something, we can all come together."

2001: THE "BOOT THE BELL" CAMPAIGN
Sunflower Catholic High School // Tampa, Florida

In 1993, farm workers in Immokalee, Florida started an organization called the Coalition of Immokalee Workers (CIW). Even though the group's members (primarily migrant workers) spoke several different languages, the CIW communicated a simple message, "Consciousness + Commitment = Change." In other words, if they educated themselves about their work and their employers, and were committed to working for better conditions, they could win.

In large numbers, the CIW confronted violent crew bosses and demanded an end to beatings in the fields. They protested and marched to demand raises, as wages had stagnated since the 1970s. CIW members also risked their lives by infiltrating slavery rings and freeing enslaved farm workers. By the end of the 1990s, however, the CIW had reached a dead-end. Farm owners claimed that the low prices paid for fruits and vegetables prevented them from raising wages above 45 cents for each 32 pound bucket picked.

Instead of giving up, in 2001, the CIW launched a boycott of Taco Bell (whose parent company, Yum! brands, is the largest restaurant corporation in the world and a major purchaser of tomatoes), demanding a penny-per-pound-raise—and a commitment to fighting slavery in Florida's fields. While labor unions and church groups around the country spread the boycott to their members, students founded a group called the Student/Farmworker Alliance (SFA) and started the "Boot the Bell" campaign to oust Taco Bell outlets from their high school and university campuses.

By 2005, when Taco Bell finally agreed to the CIW's demands, students at 25 schools, ranging from UCLA to Notre Dame University, had successfully prevented or ended contracts with Taco Bell. The list of successful campaigns also included Sunflower Catholic High School and Tampa Preparatory in Tampa, Florida; West High School in Denver, Colorado; and Carmel Catholic High School in Mundelein, Illinois; as well as Marquette Catholic High, Andrean High, and the other dozen schools affiliated with Catholic Diocese of Gary, Indiana.

In their quest to improve working conditions for farm workers, the CIW and the SFA have since won similar campaigns against McDonald's, Subway, Chipotle, Whole Foods, Burger King, and Trader Joe's, among others.

Students played important roles in all of these campaigns by challenging businesses, schools, and other institutions in their towns.

2002: NO CHILD LEFT BEHIND
United States Congress // Washington, DC

In 2002, President George W. Bush signed into law the No Child Left Behind Act (NCLB), which received support from representatives of both major political parties. Perhaps most famously, NCLB linked school funding to test score results, compelling teachers to re-orient their classrooms and "teach to the test." Since the tests focused on reading, writing, and mathematics skills, schools nationwide de-emphasized critical thinking and creativity and reduced instruction in art, music, and history.

NCLB also required that all public schools provide U.S. military recruiters with the names, addresses, and phone numbers of their students, and allow access to their students equal to that which they give to college recruiters. In 2003, just a year after NCLB passed, nearly half of the principals and superintendents polled believed that the law was either politically motivated or deliberately intended to undermine public schools.

The law's complex impacts on education are not entirely clear, in part because standardized tests are often poor measurements of knowledge. What is clear is that the law has successfully funneled tax dollars out of already struggling public schools and into the pockets of corporations. The benefit to testing companies has been estimated at between 2 billion and 7 billion dollars per year. Tutoring companies, meanwhile, whose services NCLB requires for failing schools, take in perhaps another 2 billion dollars annually.

Poorly performing schools are punished with reduced funding, and the resulting failure is then used to promote "charter schools," which are privately run—but funded with public money. Indeed, the nation's 6,000 charter schools divert massive sums of tax dollars into corporate bank accounts. For example, in Ohio alone, charter schools are a 500 million dollar per year business.

The charter school movement has promised that greed and profit would be an excellent motivation for improving schools. But despite denying teachers the right to unionize and even handpicking their students, charter schools' successes have been limited. A 2009 study found that only 17 percent of charter schools scored better than their public school counterparts, while 46 percent produced equal test scores, and 37 percent actually had test scores that were worse.

LEARNING IS MORE THAN A TEST SCORE

2003: OPPOSITION TO THE U.S. INVASION OF IRAQ
Sir Francis Drake High School // San Anselmo, California

"Support Our Troops! Bring Them Home!"

The American political climate during the U.S. invasion and occupation of Iraq was extremely hostile. President Bush and Vice President Cheney repeatedly guaranteed that the government of Iraq possessed dangerous weapons of mass destruction (WMD), and Bush further warned the world, "You are either with us, or you are with the terrorists."

This narrow mindset, combined with a culture of intense fear, allowed those who favored the war to harass and stifle the voices of those who did not. But, despite death threats and accusations that anti-war activists were terrorists and communists, the protests leading up to the invasion of Iraq in March 2003 were among the largest in world history. On February 15, between 8 and 12 million people, in over 300 cities in 60 different countries, took to the streets to protest the impending invasion.

High school students were among those who challenged the logic of the invasion. On Friday, February 21, roughly 250 students at Downtown Magnets High School in Los Angeles expressed their opposition by walking out of class and marching three miles to City Hall. The following Wednesday, nearly 100 high school students in Eugene, Oregon rallied after school and marched to the Federal Court House, where they were joined by University of Oregon students and other protestors.

On March 19, the day before the invasion, students at Sir Francis Drake High School in San Anselmo, California held a lunchtime rally at their school. Afterward, 100 students walked off campus and marched to the public library, carrying anti-war signs and chanting, "Support Our Troops, Bring Them Home!" At the library, they were met by community members, local politicians, and students from several other area schools.

Instead of engaging with the Bush Administration's phony claims about WMD, Caroline Kornfield, a student at San Domenico School, made a much simpler plea for peace. Addressing the San Anselmo crowd, she proclaimed, "We are here today to show that American youth will not condone the killing of Iraqi youth."

2004: YOUTH EMPOWERED IN THE STRUGGLE
Horlick High School // Racine, Wisconsin

"LIBERATION NOT DEPORTATION"
"TUITION EQUITY MOVES WI FORWARD"
"NO MORE SEPARATING OUR FAMILIES"

In 2004, students taking a Latino American history class at Horlick High School in Racine decided to start a student club focused on immigrant rights.

They began working with the larger organization Voces de La Frontera, and as more and more youth began joining, they pushed for in-state tuition for undocumented students at the state level (with some success) as well as the DREAM Act at the federal level. In 2010, students started their own group—Youth Empowered in the Struggle (YES). Bolstered by Wisconsin Governor Scott Walker's attacks on education, YES boasted 500 student members at twelve high schools in Milwaukee and Racine by 2012.

In addition to participating in Milwaukee's annual May Day march, YES members, with input from other youth organizations in Milwaukee, drafted a Student Bill of Rights in 2012, which they then presented to the school boards of Racine and Milwaukee.

Among its many provisions were:

"Students have a right to organize and have a voice in their school."

"Students have the right to a reasonable class size where the teacher can give adequate attention to each and every student."

"Students who are in the process of learning English deserve access to their school's curriculum with support in their native language."

"Students have a right to freedom from all forms of discrimination. This includes but is not limited to discrimination based on ethnicity, class, sex, disability, pregnancy, religion, native language, sexual orientation, gender expression, housing status, self-expression/personal style, or immigration status."

"Students have the right to teachers, staff, and administrators who understand the community in which they are working and have taken anti-racist/anti-bias training."

"Every student has the right to a school environment in which they feel safe."

Though the Racine school board voted down the bill, the Milwaukee Public School board agreed to incorporate the provisions into its student handbook.

2005: "INTELLIGENT DESIGN"
Kansas Board of Education // Topeka, Kansas

The U.S. Supreme Court outlawed bans on teaching evolution in public schools in 1968, but the ruling did not stop conservative Christian activists from trying to force their religion into public schools.

In 1981, the Louisiana state government passed a law requiring that creationism be taught alongside evolution in the state's schools. Several teachers, including Don Aguillard, a biology teacher at Acadiana High School in Lafayette, challenged it. Backed by the statements of 72 Nobel Prize winning scientists, the teachers noted that creationism was a religious belief, not a scientific theory. In 1987, the U.S. Supreme Court ruled in Edwards v. Aguillard that, indeed, laws like Louisiana's were intended to advance a particular religion and were thus unconstitutional.

Nonetheless, in 1999, the Kansas Board of Education attempted to remove evolution from the state's science curriculum. More famously, in 2005, with the backing of the (misleadingly named) Discovery Institute, members of the Kansas Board changed the state's science standards to "allow intelligent design to be presented as an alternative explanation to evolution" and "state that evolution is a theory and not a fact."

The decision became a national news story, exposing that groups in several other states, including Ohio and Oklahoma, had pursued similar changes to their curricula. Some of the news coverage even took the time to explain that the word "theory" actually has a different meaning in science than it does in everyday language. Scientists, including 38 Nobel laureates, submitted a letter explaining that unlike evolution, "intelligent design is fundamentally unscientific; it cannot be tested as scientific theory because its central conclusion is based on belief in the intervention of a supernatural agent."

The members of the Kansas Board were unswayed and voted for the changes anyway. Within a year, however, Kansas voters ousted four of the six conservative Republicans who had backed the plan, and in 2007, the new board voted to undo the changes.

But even as Kansas reclaimed science, similar policies were under consideration in as many as twenty other state.

2006: THE GREAT AMERICAN BOYCOTT
Eisenhower High School // Houston, Texas

"WE'RE NOT TERRORISTS"
"WE BUILD YOUR HOMES"
"WE ARE UNITED"

On March 27, 2006, 150 students at Houston, Texas' Eisenhower High School walked out of class and marched eight miles in order to protest at a federal immigration office.

The previous December, Republicans in the U.S. House of Representatives had passed the "Border Protection, Anti-terrorism, and Illegal Immigration Control Act of 2005." But while its title attempted to exploit Americans' fear of terrorism, the bill primarily targeted undocumented immigrants by making living in the United States illegally a felony, criminalizing humanitarian aid to immigrants, and building 700 miles of fence between the United States and Mexico.

A massive wave of immigrant rights protests swept the country in response. On March 10, over 100,000 people protested in Chicago. Later that month, as many as 500,000 demonstrated in Los Angeles. There were additional protests in Ohio, Arizona, Nevada, Texas, and elsewhere. In early April, more than 2,000,000 protestors took the streets in over 100 U.S. cities, with crowds of 300,000 or more in Chicago, Dallas, and Washington, DC. On May 1 (May Day, which is International Workers' Day), protestors organized a day of massive protests in dozens of cities across the country, including Milwaukee, Denver, San Francisco, Miami, and Atlanta. In Los Angeles, 200,000 people marched in the morning, while another 400,000 marched in the evening.

Youth played a critical role in organizing the protests. On March 27, the same day that Eisenhower High students walked out in Houston, around 1,500 students from ten different schools rallied in Dallas, while at least 14,000 students from twenty-one Los Angeles-area schools also walked out. On April 10, more than 10,000 students in Tucson, Arizona skipped class to attend a rally. And on May 1, predominantly Latino-serving schools in Chicago saw attendance drop by as much as one-third, as the youth joined the city's giant 300,000 person march.

Ultimately, the House of Representatives' bill stalled in negotiations with the U.S. Senate, and it did not become a law. However, many of its provisions have since been implemented, including the building of hundreds of miles of border fences, at a cost of several billion dollars. Though the struggle continues, the immigrant rights protests of 2006 rejuvenated May Day in the United States. The international holiday had been established to recognize the sacrifices of Chicago labor agitators in the 1880s, but mainstream celebration in the U.S. had been largely stamped out by the 1950s.

2009: THE MACARTHUR MALL PROTEST
Norfolk Collegiate High School // Norfolk, Virginia

"MALL SHOULD BE FOR ALL"
"MACARTHUR IS NOT BEING FAIR"
"1,907 STRONG AGAINST THE AGE RESTRICTIONS"

Following trends around the country, in October 2009, management at the MacArthur Center Mall in Norfolk announced a new policy targeting teenagers. Beginning later that month, anyone under eighteen would be banned from the mall after 5 p.m., unless accompanied by an adult (twenty-one years or older).

After many decades of criminalizing street corners and slashing budgets for public parks, the mall was one of the last remaining hangouts for teens in Norfolk. Youth in Norfolk, and their parents, were well aware of what was at stake. As one local school official stated, "Every kid needs a place to go...but where are they going to go now?"

At Maury High School, Norfolk Academy, and Norfolk Collegiate, students discussed the ban with their teachers and their classmates. At Collegiate, twenty students held a meeting during lunch to discuss launching a petition and starting a Facebook group. Students at Norfolk Academy also started a Facebook group and began organizing a protest at the mall. Other teens and adults launched FightMacArthur.com, proclaiming, "This rule is unprovoked, unjust, and ageist."

The day before the policy went into effect, about 40 students from various local schools picketed in front of the mall in the cold rain and confronted general manager Jim Wofford. Wofford was unphased, however. Said one fourteen-year-old protestor, "He was nice, but he didn't listen to us...he didn't respond."

During the protest, one teen remarked, "I really hope the reporters don't make this out to be something stupid...we aren't just out here goofing around." In some sense, these fears were warranted. Ultimately, teen activists were unable to accomplish anything close to a successful boycott of the mall, and Wofford and local media were quick to point out their failures. Nonetheless, in a follow-up story a year later, Wofford admitted that some of the businesses that relied on teen shoppers had indeed seen their sales figures drop.

2010: THE TEXAS TEXTBOOK SCANDAL
Texas Board of Education // Austin, Texas

Every ten years, the Texas Board of Education reviews the content of its public school textbooks. The board's recommendations shape the learning experiences of nearly 5,000,000 Texas students. They also impact students in other states who use the same books.

In 2010, the board made dozens of controversial changes to history books, despite the fact that while featuring a dentist and a real estate broker, the board included no actual historians. The board's conservative majority claimed that they were merely correcting the left-leaning bias of previous standards and re-establishing a balanced view. However, their suggestions were so over the top that the board's hearings became an international news story.

The board voted to remove Harriet Tubman, who helped runaway slaves escape to freedom, from a third grade lesson on "good citizenship." Also on the chopping block were Dolores Huerta, who co-founded the United Farm Workers union with Cesar Chavez, and the Seneca Falls Convention of 1848, the first women's rights meeting in the United States. The board's "balancing" also included removing Thomas Jefferson, the author of the Declaration of Independence (and advocate of separation of church and state), from a list of influential thinkers and replacing him with the Christian theologian John Calvin. They also decided to remove Martin Luther King Day from first graders' holiday lessons and to replace it with an emphasis on Veterans Day.

The board's additions, meanwhile, included lessons on conservative icon Phyllis Schlafly, a vocal opponent of women's rights, and the Moral Majority, an organization most clearly devoted to discriminating against women and homosexuals.

The board's most interesting decisions, however, concerned the words used in Texas textbooks. Instead of "slave trade," the board suggested a new term for the process by which 12 million Africans were violently kidnapped and brought to the Americas to do forced labor: "Triangular trade." Instead of "capitalism," the board re-named the economic system in the United States (which is guided by the capitalist class) the "free enterprise system."

After all, as one conservative board member argued, "Let's face it, capitalism does have a negative connotation...You know, 'capitalist pig!'"

SCIENCE

2011: AUSTERITY CUTS
Rufus King High School // Milwaukee, Wisconsin

"PROTECT MY FUTURE"
"KILL THE BILL"
"ATTACKING TEACHERS ATTACKS MY FUTURE"

In the wake of the economic recession of 2007, millions of Americans lost their jobs, and U.S. banks foreclosed on more than 3,000,000 homes. Rather than increasing tax revenue, however, politicians around the country seized the opportunity to slash away at public services through austerity cuts.

In 2011, Wisconsin Governor Scott Walker cut more than 1 billion dollars from public school budgets and eliminated labor union rights for teachers. Though he claimed that the changes were necessary to balance the state's budget, in fact, he had just created a deficit twice as large by offering tax breaks to corporations and the rich. In Milwaukee alone, Walker's budget forced public schools to lay off 500 employees, including 354 teachers. The Milwaukee Public School district also closed several of its schools.

The same year, Texas Governor Rick Perry pushed for $5.4 billion in public school cuts, while rejecting proposals to raise taxes or dip into the state's "rainy day" fund. Perry and his supporters claimed that the cuts would simply require schools to trim their inefficient bureaucracies. In practice, however, the state eliminated 10,000 teaching jobs (while adding 83,000 students per year) and expanded class sizes. In several cities, schools cut bus services or required students to pay much higher fees for transportation.

In both Wisconsin and Texas, teachers, students, parents, and others protested their governors' actions.

In Wisconsin, tens of thousands of people marched on Madison every day for several weeks in February and March 2011, maintaining an around-the-clock occupation of the their capitol building. On weekends, the

Madison protests ballooned to as many as 100,000 people, while additional protests were held in other cities around the state. On February 17, students at Milwaukee's Rufus King High School organized a walkout and marched four miles to join rallying students at the University of Wisconsin-Milwaukee.

On March 12, several thousand Texans marched on Austin to express their disapproval of their governor's proposals, carrying signs reading, "SAVE TEXAS SCHOOLS." According to a CBS News report, a dozen of the protestors were high school students from El Paso, who had driven twelve hours to defend public education.

2011: THE GAY-STRAIGHT ALLIANCE
Flour Bluff High School // Corpus Christi, Texas

The first Gay-Straight Alliance (GSA) was started by teacher Kevin Jennings at Concord Academy in Massachusetts in 1988. The second was started three years later by another teacher, Robert Parlin, at Newton South High School in Newton Centre, also in Massachusetts. By 2010, there were youth-led GSAs at more than 3,000 schools in the U.S.

GSAs have helped lobby for policies and laws to make schools safer, to protect lesbian, gay, bisexual, and transgender (LGBT) youth from bullying and harassment, and to ban discrimination against LGBT students. They have also provided anti-oppression training to thousands of students and teachers.

A 2007 study found that the presence of GSA groups at schools generally lowered incidents of bullying, lowered the use of homophobic language, made LGBT students feel safer, increased school attendance for LGBT youth, and helped LGBT students identify supportive adults at their schools.

However, students establishing GSAs have often faced resistance from homophobic parents, administrators, and school boards.

In 1996, the Salt Lake City Board of Education voted to eliminate all high school organizations not directly linked to classes, banning 46 clubs, in order to prevent the founding of a GSA. Student walk-outs and a 1999 lawsuit by civil liberties groups eventually overturned the ban.

In 2011, Nikki Peet, a student at Flour Bluff High School in Corpus Christi, Texas attempted to start a Gay-Straight Alliance at her school. But rather than allow the GSA, school district officials copied Salt Lake City's failed policy—banning all groups not directly linked to courses (including the Fellowship of Christian Athletes). Five months later, following a series of protests and under pressure from the ACLU of Texas, the Flour Bluff school district trustees reversed their decision.

In 2014, Elyria, Ohio parents opposing a new GSA at Elyria High School used the group's existence as a reason to lobby against "Issue 2," a tax levy to raise funds for public schools. Students rallied in support of the tax, and Issue 2 passed.

Students won in all three cases.

2012: **JUSTICE FOR TRAYVON MARTIN**
Miami, Florida

"JUSTICE FOR TRAYVON"
"BLACK IS BEAUTIFUL NOT SUSPICIOUS"
"ZIMMERMAN KILLED OUR BROTHER"
"WE ARE TRAYVON MARTIN"

In February 2012, neighborhood watch volunteer George Zimmerman shot to death seventeen-year-old Trayvon Martin, who was unarmed and walking to his father's home from a convenience store. Because Florida's "Stand Your Ground" law allows gun owners to use deadly force and claim self-defense if they are afraid, no charges were initially filed against Zimmerman.

As the story spread, so did public outrage. Professional athletes, including members of the Miami Heat basketball team, tweeted pictures of themselves wearing hooded sweatshirts—as Martin had been while walking home. Over 2,000,000 people signed an online petition calling for the District Attorney to investigate the killing, and President Barack Obama spoke publicly on the incident, noting that if he "had a son, he would look like Trayvon." Protestors in many cities held "Million Hoodie Marches" to demand justice. On March 21, Martin's parents joined thousands of marchers at a demonstration in New York City.

In Miami, where Trayvon Martin had attended high school, students walked out of 34 schools. On March 22, students at Carol City, Miami Northwestern, and Miami Norland High Schools walked out of class, demanding, "Justice for Trayvon."

The next day, at Miami Southridge, students marched to the football field and formed in the letters "T" and "M." NBC News reported that at Miami Central and Turner High, "students were seen pouring out of the school buildings and into the streets." In groups ranging from 100 to 1,000, students walked out of grade schools, middle schools, and high schools all over the city, including: Miami Norland, Miami Edison, Miami Jackson, South Miami, North Miami Beach, Homestead, Miami Northwestern, Miami Killian, Miami Carol City, American Senior, Allapattah, Country Club, Southwood, Robert Morgan Educational, North Miami, Miami Springs, Barbara Goleman, Alonzo and Tracy Mourning, Charles R. Drew, Miami Palmetto, Aventura Waterways, Carol City, Madison, COPE North, South Dade, Linda Lentin, Thomas Jefferson, and Westview.

Two weeks later, George Zimmerman was indicted for the murder of Trayvon Martin.

Using the defense that he himself was the victim, Zimmerman was found not guilty that July.

2012: MAY DAY Paul Robeson High School // Brooklyn, New York

"WE ARE THE 99%"
"WE ARE STUDENTS, NOT STATISTICS"
"ROBESON UNITE— WALK 4 MAY DAY"

Following brutal attacks on Occupy Wall Street demonstrations in the Fall and Winter of 2011, OWS activists called for a day of protest on May 1, 2012. The "99%" in cities all over the country responded with a variety of actions. In April, students at Paul Robeson High School in Brooklyn began organizing a May Day walk-out to protest city officials' decision to close their school.

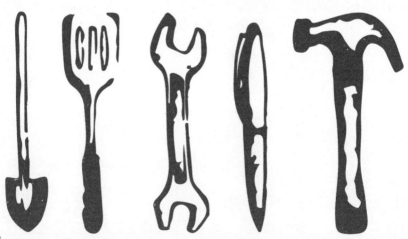

They issued the following call:

"Dear New York City,
We the students of public education are here to inform you about the injustice that is taking place in our school system: the privatization of our school system, the budget cuts, lack of appropriate leadership, malicious closings, phase-outs against community wishes, cell phone policies, overcrowded classes, and abuse of safe rooms, over-policing of our schools and criminalization of our youth.

We feel that these issues are setting up our students for failure, and we demand a change. We believe that trying to control our schools is just another symptom of the blatant racism in our country, similar to the government's response to the senseless killing of Trayvon Martin.
Because of this, our first action will be a mass student walk-out on May 1st, at 12 p.m., to Fort Greene Park. We will be holding teach-ins, teen summits, and other peaceful events.

Please add your name to our letter and support us in our struggle for our education.

Signed,
Student Leadership, Paul Robeson High School"

On May Day, 93 Paul Robeson students were joined by community members and teachers as they marched through their community. The students were suspended for their actions. Said Shanique Williams, one of the protestors, "I thought we would fall back and just let it happen. But we're not. We're standing up. I'm proud of my school."

At the end of the year, Paul Robeson High, named after the famous African-American singer, actor, and radical activist, was closed.

2012: MAY DAY, CONTINUED
Philadelphia, Pennsylvania
Redwood City, California
Portland, Oregon

On the evening of May 1, 2012—the same day that Paul Robeson students walked out of class in Brooklyn—roughly 300 students, parents, and teachers in the Drexel Hill area of Philadelphia, Pennsylvania also rallied to protest a 4 million dollar budget cut that included the firing of 57 teachers in the district's physical education, music, art, library, technology, and foreign language programs.

Earlier, 30 Sequoia High School students in Redwood City, California also walked out of class, waving signs reading

"STUDENT STRIKE" "STOP CUTTING OUR SCHOOL BUDGETS" "THE NEXT 99%" "STOP CHARTER SCHOOL FUNDS"

Meanwhile, hundreds of public school students in Portland, Oregon marched on both city hall and school district headquarters to protest budget cuts and school closings. Their chants included, "No More Cuts! Save Our Schools!" "No More Excuses! No More Cuts!" and "We Love Our Teachers!"

The students were joined by Occupy activists, community members, and parents, and they were greeted by Portland Mayor Sam Adams and Superintendent Carole Smith, who listened to their grievances.

Paul Wells, a Portland high school student, told the city newspaper,

"I've lived through these austerity measures at school. I've seen my education go more and more downhill."

MAY DAY

109

2012: THE PINK SLIP PROTEST
Point Loma High School // San Diego, California

In the Spring of 2012, the San Diego Unified School District announced that it would lay off more than 1,500 teachers (out of about 7,000 total) in order to close a 100 million dollar budget deficit. The plan would also grow kindergarten through third grade classes from twenty-four to thirty-one students.

On June 6, more than 2,000 students marched out of Point Loma High School in support of the 25 Point Loma teachers who were fired. Many teachers and students wore pink that day, to represent the "pink slips" given to teachers.

Two days later, on Friday, June 8, more than 100 students at Lincoln High School also walked out, to protest the firing of 32 of their teachers.

On June 12, students at Hearst Elementary marked the last day of classes by protesting outside of their school. They were joined by teachers and parents.

2012: THE EAGLE SCOUT RESIGNATIONS
Boy Scouts of America Headquarters //
Irving, Texas

In July 2012, a leadership committee of the Boy Scouts of America (BSA) reviewed its membership policies and announced that the organization, unlike its Girl Scout counterpart, would continue to exclude openly gay participants, as members or as adult leaders. Following the announcement, dozens of Eagle Scouts (those who had earned scouting's highest rank) all over the country began returning their medals to the Boy Scouts' national office in Irving, Texas. Though a BSA spokesperson claimed that the office had received only a "few" medals, in less than a year, more than 200 Eagle Scouts posted letters explaining their decisions to eaglebadges.tumblr.com, and local and national media picked up the story.

The letters are both inspiring and heart-breaking. In them, scouts, ranging from recent Eagle recipients to those who had earned the award many decades earlier, explain how much their experiences have meant to them and how outraged they are by the BSA's ban.

Excerpts from three of them:

> "...How sad that an organization that teaches leadership has chosen to relinquish the lead in one of the most important civil rights issues of our time..."

> "...Your current stance is one of discrimination and intolerance. My country recognizes equal rights for homosexual partners; you have chosen to characterize gays as somehow deviant. Duty to others means helping others, and doing good deeds. One's sexual orientation does not make a person less human or in need of care, love, and support...As an Eagle Scout, I challenge you to live up to the Scout Oath and to welcome gays into Scouting's ranks..."

"...I act in solidarity with all gay boys, fathers, and mothers who will no longer be allowed to participate in this organization and its activities which I, as a boy who was not yet even considering his sexual orientation, was accepted into and benefitted from. I act to prevent the indoctrination of assumedly heterosexual boys and families who might accept BSA's current ruling as anything more substantial than sanctioned ignorance (at best) or institutionalized homophobia (at worst)..."

In 2013, the BSA reversed its position, announcing that openly gay youth would be allowed into scouting. The ban on openly gay adult leaders, however, remains in effect.

2012: THE REBELS ON THE GRIDIRON
South Plantation High School //
Plantation, Florida

In Fall 2012, the *New York Times* ran an article about South Plantation High School's third-string quarterback (and eventual homecoming queen), Erin DiMeglio. She was the first female quarterback to play in a Florida high school football game, but DiMeglio was only one of the roughly 1,500 girls who play high school football in the U.S. each year.

Many of them are kickers—a position well-suited for athletes with smaller frames. Pinckney Community High School's Brianna Amat, for example, kicked a game-winning field goal for her Michigan high school team—and was named homecoming queen on the same night. Marine City High School kicker Olivia Viney kicked 61 extra points during the 2013 season, including seven during a win in the Michigan state championship game. At least three women have become place kickers for college football teams. Female football players have also excelled at other positions, however.

During the 1981 season, fourteen-year-old Tami Maida shared quarterbacking duties on the JV squad for Philomath High School in Oregon.

In 1998, Jellico High School running back Jessica Schultz became the first girl on a Tennessee varsity football team to score a touchdown.

Three years later, Sami Grisafe of Redlands High School became the first female quarterback to compete in a California Division I High School football game.

In 2007, Holley Mangold played offensive line for Archbishop Alter High School in Kettering, Ohio—and later became an Olympic weightlifter.

During the 2011 season, Lisa Spangler was the starting middle linebacker for Fort Vancouver High School in Vancouver, Washington, and Monique Howard played right tackle for Pershing High School in Detroit, Michigan.

The same year, Andrea Marsh played defensive back for Panama High School in Panama, New York and recorded 55 tackles and four interceptions.

2012: THE "WORK TO THE RULES" PROTEST
James Campbell High School // Honolulu, Hawaii

"YOU CAN'T PUT STUDENTS

"FAIR DEAL FOR STUDENTS

Copying governors all over the country, in 2012, Hawaii Governor Neil Abercrombie announced that rather than negotiate with teachers' unions, he would instead dictate his final contract offer, which included cuts in wages and increases in health insurance premiums. If the teachers refused, Abercrombie threatened, the only other solution would be widespread lay-offs.

In response, teachers in Hawaii held a series of demonstrations in October and November. Teachers in Honolulu announced that while they would not go on strike, they would "work to the rules" to protest the Governor. Like New York teachers in 1950, they planned to work 8 a.m. to 3 p.m., as dictated by the specific terms of their contracts. They would not participate in the after-school activities they normally did voluntarily.

FIRST IF YOU PUT TEACHERS LAST"

AND TEACHERS"

On November 15, teachers from Campbell High School worked "to the rules" and rallied along a busy street. They held signs asking for honks of support and wore T-shirts reading, "YOU CAN'T PUT STUDENTS FIRST IF YOU PUT TEACHERS LAST." They were joined by parents and students, boosting their numbers to as many as 500. They carried signs reading, "FAIR DEAL FOR STUDENTS AND TEACHERS" and "GOVERNOR, WHERE'S OUR CONTRACT?"

Said one Campbell senior, "I just hope they know that even if we're kind of a pain, that we do care about them and we do support them."

"We came to support the teachers because they don't get enough pay for everything they do, and we just want them to be paid fairly," offered another.

The next April, teachers and the state reached agreement on a new four-year contract.

2013: THE SIMSBURY HIGH SCHOOL VEGETARIAN CLUB
Simsbury High School // Simsbury, Connecticut

In 2012, students at Thomas S. Wootton High School in Rockville, Maryland started a group called the Animal Rights / Vegan and Vegetarian Club to educate students about the benefits of a meatless diet. As one founding member explained to the local newspaper, raising animals for food generates more greenhouse emissions than using cars or planes does.

The next year, students at Simsbury High School in Simsbury, Connecticut also formed a vegetarian club, with the goal of "helping animals and promoting a healthy dietary choices." The group's events included a bake sale (with vegan options) to raise money for the adoption of a "rescue duck" at a farm sanctuary. The group also participated in "National Meatout Day" by lobbying their school to offer a vegan lunch option on March 20 and to publish vegetarian recipes on its website. On Meatout Day, group members sat at a table throughout lunch, offering students who chose the vegan option the opportunity to enter a raffle. The students also wore T-shirts reading, "SHS VEGETARIAN CLUB SUPPORTS NATIONAL MEATOUT DAY—TAKE THE CHALLENGE."

Perhaps the most successful campaign to reduce American meat consumption, however, is the Meatless Mondays program, which has been adopted by dozens of grade schools, high schools, and colleges all over the U.S. By promoting a once a week vegetarian diet, Meatless Mondays aims to limit the risk of cancer, fight diabetes, reduce the risk of heart disease, reduce fossil fuel dependence, reduce water usage, and reduce greenhouse gases. With so many potential benefits, the program has attracted participating school districts from Arlington, Virginia and Detroit, Michigan to Santa Cruz, California and Covington, Kentucky.

The Meatless Mondays campaign has not been universally embraced, however. In 2012, the U.S. Department of Agriculture (USDA) distributed a newsletter to its employees that mentioned the merits of the program, but officials quickly retracted the newsletter after receiving criticism from the National Cattlemen's Beef Association and Kansas Senator Jerry

Moran (who had received hundreds of thousands of dollars in contributions from the beef and dairy industries). The next year, the cafeteria of the U.S. House of Representatives announced that it would participate in Meatless Mondays, but it, too, was forced to abandon the plan under pressure from beef industry lobbyists.

2013: THE GREENWICH DRESS CODE PROTEST
Greenwich High School // Greenwich, Connecticut

"GHS BODY SHAMES"
"MY BODY, MY RULES"
"I LOVE MY BODY"

In May 2013, after being chastised by Greenwich High School officials for her clothing, Grace DiChristina and her sister, Patrice, organized a one-day protest and called for a committee of students and staff to review the school's dress code. Grace felt that school officials' statements were intended to make her feel ashamed of her body. She said, "I just didn't feel the need to change or cover myself...I'm not going to accept shame for something that I'm not ashamed of."

The school's dress code required that students dress "within reasonable limits," but those limits were vague and subjective, allowing teachers and administrators to decide whose clothing was disruptive and whose was not. According to Grace DiChristina, these standards were not applied to all students equally.

On May 28, she and her sister—and about 50 of their friends—arrived at school wearing T-shirts on which they had boldly written protest slogans. They included, "GHS BODY SHAMES," "MY BODY, MY RULES," and "I LOVE MY BODY."

Greenwich High School Principal Chris Winters was unswayed, but with media attention focused on the school, he agreed to meet with the protestors and discuss the school's policies.

2013: THE BELTON HIGH SCHOOL SALUTATORIAN SPEECH
Belton High School // Belton, Texas

Belton High School's senior class salutatorian Mitch Anderson gave a speech during the school's 2013 graduation ceremony.

In it, he encouraged his classmates to be brave and to be themselves. *He also revealed for the first time something about himself.*

He said,

"You may think that hiding yourself is worth some superficial praise by society, or you can choose to learn that being who you are is vastly more important...

I myself am guilty of self-doubt, relying on others to give my life definition. But that time has passed, and I feel the moment has arrived for me to be publically true to my personal identity. So now, I can say, I'm gay. It is both a significant portion of who I am and an inconsequential aspect. It's as natural and effortless to me as breathing. I couldn't change myself even if I wanted, and believe me, I have.

I have been bullied a lot. I've been called unspeakable things and relegated to a place of lower class... There were moments when I believed I was next to nothing. But I learned that what others think of you is not nearly as meaningful as what you think of yourself...

The world could use a little bit more love. Let us all not be so quick to judge. We ought to be a bit kinder to others. Be not afraid of what you do not know, because more often than not, it's probably incredibly similar to what you know. And when you disagree with someone, hate is not a form of love. Think for a moment about what damage your words would do before speaking...

Please, embrace self-empowerment. You gain confidence, an unswerving belief that you matter and the ability of your existence to make an indelible mark on the world. You gain compassion and empathy. You will love and be loved. Most importantly, you will finally start living the life that you were always meant to live.

I would be remiss, however, if I failed to incorporate a Harry Potter reference to the theme of my speech, so I will. Be a Luna Lovegood, not a Pansy Parkinson. Be a little bit strange and off-kilter, and not so desperate to be popular...Find fellowship with everyone, not those you have preordained."

2013: CENSORSHIP ON EVERY PAGE
Office of the Governor // Indianapolis, Indiana

In 2012, former Indiana Governor Mitch Daniels was named President of Purdue University by the Board of Trustees, whose members he had previously appointed. Publicly, Daniels emphasized a belief in the importance of academic freedom and freedom of speech. But the following year, the Associated Press obtained e-mails from his time as governor. They revealed Daniels' attempts in 2009 and 2010 to censor the curriculum of Indiana's K-12 students and to shape the materials used to train teachers. Specifically, Daniels sought to ban the use of the book *A People's History of the United States* by historian Howard Zinn.

Daniels took issue with Zinn's book because it focused on American history's underdogs: Native Americans instead of Christopher Columbus, African slaves instead of slave owners, and factory workers instead of industrialists. Though Daniels himself had no training as a historian, he called Zinn's book "disinformation that misstates American history on every page."

Daniels also celebrated Zinn's death, rejoicing, "This terrible anti-American academic has finally passed away." Zinn's anti-American credentials included serving as a bombardier in World War II, being fired for supporting his African-American students during the Civil Rights Movement, and being an outspoken voice for peace during the Vietnam and Iraq wars.

Daniels' behind-the-scenes censorship did not negatively impact his position as the head of a major research university. However, after the Associated Press article about it ran, eBook sales of *A People's History* nearly doubled. A few months later, teachers, activists, and students also held "read-ins" at Purdue and several other schools to celebrate Zinn's work.

Zinn, who died in 2010, was unable to respond to Governor Daniels personally, but he made his position clear twenty years earlier when he wrote, "If those in charge of our society—politicians, corporate executives, and owners of press and television—can dominate our ideas, they will be secure in their power."

Howard Zinn's books, which Mitch Daniels does not want young people to read, include: *Disobedience and Democracy*, *You Can't Be Neutral on a Moving Train*, and *A Young People's History of the United States*. Zinn also produced *The People Speak*, in which well-known actors read the speeches and statements of dissidents and rebels from throughout U.S. history.

2013: CASSIDY LYNN CAMPBELL'S HOMECOMING CORONATION
Marina High School // Huntington Beach, California

According to a 2011 national poll, 78 percent of transgender K-12 students experience harassment at their schools, and 35 percent experience physical assault. In August 2013, the California state legislature, responding to pressure from a variety of civil liberties organizations and LGBT teens, passed a new law to address this discrimination and grant transgender students the right to participate in athletics and use restrooms according to their gender.

However, the idea of transgender rights was not universally embraced.

Fox News hosts called the California laws "very scary" and described them as "social engineering run amok." Just a few days later, a group of men shouting homophobic slurs beat to death transgender woman Islan Nettles on a New York City street. According to a study by the National Coalition of Anti-Violence Programs, more than a dozen transgender women in the U.S. were murdered in hate crimes in the year prior.

In September 2013, students at Marina High School in Huntington Beach defied transphobic bullies and bigots by nominating transgender teen Cassidy Lynn Campbell for homecoming queen. In anticipation, she remarked, "I'm a girl and if my school could recognize me as what I've always wanted the world to recognize me as my entire life, then it would be such an accomplishment." The next week, her classmates did just that. She won.

After her victory, Campbell was viciously harassed through social media, but the sixteen-year-old understood that her coronation was part of a much larger struggle for social justice. As she told news reporters, "I realized that it wasn't for me anymore and I was doing this for so many other people...not just the county, and not just the state, but the nation and possibly even the world...I am so proud to win this, not just for me but for everyone out there."

The same year, students at the University of Northern Iowa also elected a transgender student as their homecoming queen.

2013: THE EASTSIDE CATHOLIC SOLIDARITY PROTESTS
Eastside Catholic High School // Sammamish, Washington

"21st CENTURY CATHOLICS FOR A 21st CENTURY CHURCH"
"GOD IS LOVE, STOP THE HATE"
"WE LOVE YOU MR. Z"
"SAME SEX = SAME LOVE"
"NO FREEDOM TIL WE'RE EQUAL"

In November 2012, voters in Washington approved Referendum 74, which legalized marriage equality. The law took effect in December, and over the next year, several thousand same-sex couples were married.

Among them were Dana Jergens and his partner Mark Zmuda, a vice principal and swim coach at Eastside Catholic High School in Sammamish. But while Referendum 74 granted all Washington residents the legal right to get married, it did not protect them from retaliation by their employers. In December 2013, officials at Eastside Catholic discovered Zmuda's marriage and forced him to resign. School officials made clear that they were not discriminating against Zmuda for his sexuality—only for his marriage, which violated Catholic doctrine.

In response to Zmuda's firing, hundreds of Eastside students flooded the school cafeteria and gymnasium before walking out in protest, compelling the school to close early for winter break. Support for Zmuda then spread to other area Catholic schools, and protestors rallied at Sammamish City Hall, at the offices of the Archdiocese of Seattle, and at an Eastside High swim meet. Seattle Mayor-elect Ed Murray joined protestors at the Archdiocese. The story became international news, and an online petition launched by Eastside Catholic senior class president Bradley Strode received 35,000 signatures within a month.

Mark Zmuda was not allowed to return to Eastside High, but in July 2014, he was hired as associate principal and athletic director at nearby Mercer Island High School.

2014: OPERATION: GUINEA PIG
Providence, Rhode Island

"I'M A STUDENT, NOT AN EXPERIMENT"
"STOP PLAYING GAMES WITH MY FUTURE"
"NO MORE NECAP"

In January 2014, students from Providence's Hope High School, the Met School, and Dr. Jorge Alvarez High School visited the Rhode Island Statehouse wearing paper mouse ears, pipe cleaner whiskers, and guinea pig masks.

The protest, which they dubbed "Operation: Guinea Pig," was organized by a citywide student activist group, the Providence Student Union (PSU). It targeted state representatives' decision to link high school graduation to students' scores on standardized tests, the New England Common Assessment Program (NECAP).

Carrying signs reading, "NO MORE NECAP" and "I'M A STUDENT, NOT AN EXPERIMENT," the students rallied on the statehouse steps. As one student explained, "We are dressed like guinea pigs and lab rats [because] that is how we are being treated." As an alternative to lawmakers' attempt to reduce students to a test score, PSU demanded more art courses, smaller class sizes, and more accessible public transit.

With statehouse officials and media representatives watching, the students performed a political skit and began chanting, "High stakes testing is not right! That is why we have to fight!"

The next month (in the February cold), PSU organized a three-mile march to draw attention to the city's policy that only students living more than three miles from their schools could use public transportation for free.

The protest worked. The students won.

In response to their campaign, the school board reduced the radius to 2.5 miles, providing bus access to 800 students. The board also voted to re-work some of the NECAP testing requirements.

2014: THE PORTLAND STUDENT UNION
Jefferson High School // Portland, Oregon

"FIGHTING FOR THE SCHOOLS WE DESERVE"
"SUPPORT TEACHERS!"
"SOLIDARITY FOREVER"

In November 2013, after eight months of negotiations, contract talks between the Portland Public Schools and the teachers' union, the Portland Association of Teachers, reached an impasse. Among the key sticking points was whether or not to lift caps on class sizes. As the conflict escalated, members of the citywide Portland Student Union mobilized to support their teachers.

On Friday, December 13, 2013, dozens of students at Woodrow Wilson High School walked out of class, despite a warning e-mail from their principal. Students rallied along a nearby street, holding signs reading, "HONK FOR SMALLER CLASS SIZES," "SUPPORT TEACHERS!" and "NO IFS, NO BUTS, NO EDUCATION CUTS."

On Friday, January 10, as many as 200 students at Jefferson High School held a walk-out, marching behind a banner that read, "PDX STUDENT UNION, SOLIDARITY FOREVER" and carrying signs, such as "FIGHTING FOR THE SCHOOLS WE DESERVE," "SUPPORT OUR TEACHERS," and "DON'T FORCE A STRIKE."

The following Monday, students from several schools protested outside of a school district meeting. Their chants of "If you strike, we do too!" were so loud that the meeting was cancelled.

On Wednesday, February 5, as teachers prepared to vote on whether or not to go on strike, students at Jefferson and Wilson High School held lunch-time rallies, while students at Cleveland, Lincoln, Grant, and Madison

High Schools walked out. Teachers approved a strike, but, with just days to spare, the two sides reached an agreement.

Under the terms of the new contract, the school district agreed to hire 150 new teachers and to keep the current caps on class sizes.

The students and their teachers won.

2014: THE CENSORING OF THE CARDINAL COLUMNS
Fond du Lac High School // Fond du Lac, Wisconsin

"FREE OUR VOICES" "GIVE US OUR VOICE BACK" "STOP THE UNFAIR CENSORSHIP"

In February 2014, the Fond du Lac High School student newspaper, Cardinal Columns, published Tanvi Kumar's article "The Rape Joke: Surviving Rape in a Culture That Won't Let You."

Angered after hearing a rape-themed joke in the school hallways, Kumar interviewed several rape survivors (with the promise of anonymity), polled students about sexual violence, and directed readers to a local resource center for survivors. She and other editors also included a brief piece contrasting students' responses to poll questions with national statistics on sexual assault, concluding, "By the time you finish reading this, eleven people will have been sexually assaulted. That's the rape joke. Now ask yourself—did you laugh?"

Kumar was awarded the Voices of Courage Award by the Wisconsin Coalition Against Sexual Assault, and the article won eleven other awards from the Northeastern Wisconsin Scholastic Press Association. The piece was widely discussed in Fond du Lac High classes, and a teacher even reached out to Kumar to share her own experiences with sexual violence.

However, not everyone was pleased with the article, or how it represented the school. A few weeks after its publication, Superintendent James Sebert directed Principal Jon Wiltzius to inform the newspapers' editors that all future content would have to be pre-approved by administrators. According to Kumar, Wiltzius told student journalists that their articles should be "more positive." For the April issue of the paper, Wiltzius demanded that students remove a photograph of a student with duct-tape over his mouth (to illustrate the new limits on free speech) and eliminate the word "faggot" from an article on bullying.

In response to the administration's censorship policy, students launched a petition, which received over 5,000 signatures. Then, on May 1, 60 students wearing shirts and bracelets reading, "FREE OUR VOICE," held a sit-in outside of the school's main office. With news media and some supportive parents present, administrators moved the protestors out of the hallway and listened to their grievances. They then began issuing truancy and loitering tickets to those who refused to return to class. The last ten remaining protestors continued their demonstration outside of the school in the rain.

Two days later, Principal Wiltzius announced his resignation. The school board promised to review the censorship policy in the near future.

2014: THE OVERLAND HIGH SCHOOL SOLIDARITY TWEET
Overland High School // Aurora, Colorado

"#LOVEMYTEAM"
"#LETSAMAHPLAY"

In March 2014, referees refused to allow **Overland High School** soccer player Samah Aidah to play while wearing a hijab (Islamic headscarf).

Outraged by this expression of intolerance, the entire team and coaching staff arrived for the next game wearing headscarves in solidarity.

Before playing, they posed for a photo, which was re-tweeted more than 20,000 times.

Appropriately, Overland High School's teams are known as the "Trailblazers."

2014: THE NEWARK STUDENTS UNION
Newark, New Jersey

"SAVE OUR SCHOOLS" "PARENTS, TEACHERS, STUDENTS UNITED TO SAVE OUR SCHOOLS" "WE'RE MORE THAN JUST A STATISTIC"

In 2013, Newark Superintendent Cami Anderson announced the "One Newark Plan" to revamp the school district through a combination of centralizing enrollment, closing and re-organizing schools, laying off teachers, emphasizing standardized testing, and "partnering" with privately run charter schools. Critics saw in her plan the same combination of testing, privatization, and instability that had been failing in cities all over the country for more than a decade. Anderson's insistence that all schools meet the same standards or risk closure also seemed to punish both teachers and students at schools with greater socioeconomic challenges.

In April 2014, after conducting a series of town hall meetings and surveys, several Newark groups, including the local chapter of the NAACP and the local teachers' union unveiled their own plan, the "Newark Promise." In contrast to Anderson's plan, the Newark Promise calls for local control and initiative, assessment that takes into account more than testing, a curriculum that "emphasizes active learning, the arts, physical outlets, and apprenticeship programs in addition to college readiness," and a "positive school climate that uses law enforcement as a last result [and] prevents bullying."

Three days later, members of the Newark Students Union (NSU) held a protest at a Board of Education meeting. While dozens of students rallied outside of the building, nine others started a sit-in that effectively shut down the meeting. Their demands included Anderson's resignation, local control over the education system, fair and full funding of schools, and a moratorium on school closures. Though she listened to their demands, Anderson accused the students of being "coached by adults." They responded that "autonomy" was an important concept to their organization and that they had not been coached. Rather, they shut down the meeting as a means of escalating their campaign. Students had already spoken at previous meetings and organized a district-wide student walkout the previous month.

During the occupation, the students received a supportive visit from Mayor-elect Ras Baraka (who had run on a platform opposing Anderson's plan), and the next day they ended their sit-in after being promised a meeting with Anderson and State Education Commissioner David Hespe.

They left that meeting unsatisfied, vowing to continue to fight for their education.

2014: CLIMATE CHANGE AND THE KEYSTONE XL PIPELINE
Nathan Hale High School // Seattle, Washington

"PROTECT OUR FUTURE, NO KEYSTONE XL"
"PROTECT OUR ONLY HOME"
"STOP THE KEYSTONE PIPELINE"

On April 29, 2014, a few dozen students from Nathan Hale High School and Garfield High School marched through downtown Seattle and conducted a sit-in that blocked the front entrance to the Henry M. Jackson Federal Building.

Chanting and carrying signs reading, "STOP THE PIPELINE" and "NO KXL," the students urged President Barack Obama not to approve permits for the Keystone XL pipeline, which would deliver sludgy oil from Alberta, Canada's Tar Sands to refineries in Texas. As Garfield senior Erasmus Baxter told a local reporter, "The effects of climate change aren't just abstract. It's something that's going to affect us and our children. And we need to make a concrete step."

In addition to destroying the local ecosystem, harvesting oil from the Tar Sands also requires the violation of indigenous treaty rights and jeopardizes the drinking water of millions of Americans. Former NASA scientist James Hansen has described the climate impact of exploiting the region's oil as "game over" for the planet.

But the Tar Sands and the Keystone XL pipeline represent hundreds of billions of dollars in potential profits for oil companies, making support for the project an attractive position for politicians.

Opposition to the project has also been widespread, however. In 2011, protestors held a two-week-long sit-in in front of the White House, leading to 1,000 arrests. In 2012, protestors in Texas were arrested for locking themselves to machinery and halting construction. In April 2014, Nebraska ranchers and American Indian activists formed the "Cowboy Indian Alliance" and marched together through the streets of Washington, DC.

The futures of both the pipeline and the planet are still being debated.

2014: LIBERTY AND JUSTICE FOR ALL
Needville High School // Needville, Texas

In 1943, the U.S. Supreme Court ruled in West Virginia State Board of Education v. Barnette that Americans' free speech rights protected students from being forced to recite the Pledge of Allegiance or to salute the American flag.

Nonetheless, in May 2014, Needville High School sophomore Mason Michalec was given a two-day in-school suspension for silently refusing to stand for the Pledge of Allegiance, the Texas Pledge of Allegiance, or the Moment of Silence (Texas' way of injecting prayer into public schools). Needville High's principal also warned Michalec that he would receive a two-day suspension for each additional infraction.

According to the fifteen-year-old, his protest was directed at the U.S. government's domestic spying programs. As he told a local news station, "I don't agree with the NSA spying on us." Specifically, he cited government efforts to collect Americans' internet activity and account information, such as the Cyber Intelligence Sharing and Protection Act (CISPA) being debated in Congress.

Some local residents called his behavior "wrong" and "disrespectful to the flag and those folks who gave their lives for him." One local offered, "If you live in the United States, the greatest country in the world, you should support the United States." Though Michalec had said nothing derogatory about U.S. soldiers, another local added, "The soldiers are out there, they're doing their job, and he should stand up."

But one local military veteran defended his protest, calling Michalec "well-informed" and telling reporters, "I'm not real big on flag-burning or anything like that, but this country is a free country and we're free to do what we want."

2014: TEACHER APPRECIATION...AND THE BOUNCY HOUSE
Washington High School // Kansas City, Kansas

Twelve days before Washington High School seniors were set to graduate, school administrators announced a series of changes to the school's end of the year rituals. They included instituting a more formal dress code for graduation, shortening the graduation ceremony by removing a "Teacher Appreciation Walk," eliminating a school talent show, and canceling a "bouncy house" at the senior picnic.

Outraged, senior Ebony Germany drafted a letter to administrators that listed students' grievances. It concluded, "After thirteen years of hard work and dedication...this feels like a slap in the face...we can't even give our teachers a hug of appreciation, it's sad." She then circulated copies of the letter to her classmates, leaving a blank space where each could insert his or her name, before delivering it to school officials.

When seniors then began an impromptu protest in the hallway outside of the school office, administrators called in police. Said one student who was in the office to pay his 50-dollar graduation fee, "They started pulling out mace, they started saying that we had to get out." After police cleared the hallways, administrators met with senior class representatives. Though it was too late to organize a talent show, administrators offered a compromise.

They granted the students' top demand by adding the Teacher Appreciation Walk to the graduation ceremony. They also promised that if a bouncy house could be found on such short notice, it would be rented for the picnic.

2014: DEMONSTRATIONS IN SOLIDARITY WITH RAPE SURVIVORS
Calhoun High School // Calhoun, Georgia

"NO MEANS NO"
"SPEAK UP AGAINST RAPE"

On the night of May 10, 2014, after Calhoun High School's prom, three Calhoun seniors sexually assaulted one of their classmates at a party. Local police launched an investigation, interviewing as many as 50 potential witnesses and identifying the suspects.

In prominent incidents two years earlier, popular teenage boys were accused of raping intoxicated girls in Steubenville, Ohio and Maryville, Missouri. In those cases, many local community members and news reporters viciously blamed the victims and defended the perpetrators. In Steubenville, school officials attempted to cover up the crime, and in Maryville, prosecutors dropped the investigation until it became national news. National public outrage played significant roles in compelling law enforcement to pursue both cases.

By contrast, in Calhoun, students and parents organized a series of protests outside of the school to demand justice. They held signs reading, "NO MEANS NO," "SPEAK UP AGAINST RAPE," and "THEIR DAUGHTER TODAY, YOUR DAUGHTER TOMORROW." As one protesting parent told a local newspaper, "We don't want this to be swept under the rug...We're here in support of the victim to let her know she is not alone. There are people in the community behind her."

At Calhoun High's graduation ceremony on May 23, the loudest cheers were in support of the survivor, and many graduating seniors wore blue ribbons on their gowns in solidarity.

The three suspects were not allowed to participate in the graduation and were officially charged with aggravated sexual battery and drinking alcohol under age.

2014: THE FREE RAUL PROTEST
Salem South High School / Salem, Oregon

"LET RAUL WALK!"
"#FREERAUL"

At noon on June 4, 2014, several dozen students walked out of Salem South High School to rally and demand that their classmate Raul Villarreal be allowed to participate in the graduation ceremony two days later. Said one student, "I think [administrators] are trying to make an example of Raul. I think they're making an example of the wrong person."

At prom a few weeks earlier, Villarreal and his friends had been confronted by administrators and police, who accused the students of smoking marijuana. Though they denied the charges, officials continued to pressure them. Said Villarreal, "I felt bullied and harassed...They told me it wasn't illegal, told me [confessing] would make things easier. I thought, 'If I say yes, will you leave me alone?' I was really nervous and I didn't know what was going on. I honestly was not expecting this."

Villarreal eventually agreed with their accusations and was kicked out of the dance. But though he said it was a false confession—and a subsequent drug test came back negative—he was suspended from school for five days and told that he could not participate in graduation.

In addition to the walkout, students decorated their cars with supportive slogans and 600 students signed a petition on his behalf.

Administrators refused to reconsider, but Villarreal expressed his gratitude for his classmates' support.

2014: THE WILSON HIGH SCHOOL COUNTER-DEMONSTRATION
Woodrow Wilson High School // Washington, DC

"WILSON'S GOT PRIDE"
"LOVE CONQUERS HATE"
"I HAVE TWO MOMS AND LIFE IS GOOD"

Aside from the Ku Klux Klan, the Westboro Baptist Church (WBC) of Topeka, Kansas is probably the most well-known hate group in the United States. Carrying homophobic signs reading "GOD HATES FAGS," "FAGS DIE, GOD LAUGHS," and "AIDS KILLS FAGS," the Westboro Baptists have picketed the funerals of soldiers, the sites of national tragedies, and essentially anywhere else that they felt would attract attention.

In 2002, ten Westboro Baptists traveled to Dover, New Hampshire to protest Dover High School students' decision to vote two girls their senior class' "best couple." The school's principal advised the yearbook committee to feature a heterosexual couple instead, but he was over-ruled by the superintendent. When the Westboro Baptists arrived in Dover, they were greeted by counter-protestors, including many Dover High School students.

In 2007, Westboro Baptists arrived in York, Pennsylvania to protest York Suburban Senior High School's production of The Laramie Project, a play that examines the brutal 1998 murder of Matthew Shepard near Laramie, Wyoming. There, too, high schoolers rallied to express their disapproval of the WBC's bigotry.

In June 2014, the Westboro Baptists went to Washington, DC to protest Wilson High School's openly gay principal. But Wilson's Gay-Straight Alliance and student government had been busy making preparations. One thousand counter-protestors welcomed the dozen or so WBC members with tolerance, love, and a little bit of humor.

Some protestors countered the WBC's heinous message with signs reading, "LOVE ALWAYS WINS," "PEOPLE ARE EQUAL!" and "LIVE AND LET LOVE."

Others mocked the WBC for having the audacity to speak on behalf a deity, holding signs like "GOD HATES FROGS," "GOD HATES REPORT CARDS," and "GOD HATES BACON."

2014: **THE FIGHT FOR HISTORY (AND FOR THE FUTURE)** *Evergreen High School // Golden, Colorado*

"HISTORY SHOULDN'T BE CENSORED"

"FIGHTING FOR MY FUTURE"

"U CAN'T BRAINWASH ALL OF US"

"HOW'S THIS FOR CIVIL DISOBEDIENCE?"

In 2014, conservatives took control of the school board of Jefferson County, Colorado. In addition to demonizing teachers and funneling tax dollars to corporations through charter schools, they also sought to re-shape the Advanced Placement (AP) U.S. history curriculum to "promote patriotism" and "respect for authority," while downplaying inequality and discouraging civil disobedience.

On Friday, September 19, the plan began to backfire, however, when dozens of teachers at Standley Lake and Conifer high schools protested by calling in sick, forcing the schools to close for the day.

The following week, students put civil disobedience back into their curriculum. On Monday, 250 students at Evergreen High School walked out of class and protested at school board headquarters. The next day, 400 students at Arvada High School, 500 at Arvada West, and hundreds more at Pomona High, Ralston Valley High, Chatfield, and Golden High also walked out.

By the end of the week, protests had spread to Columbine, Lakewood, Bear Creek, and Dakota Ridge high schools, as well, and the students' fight had become a national news story.

Censoring history sound like brain

CONCLUSION

The clashes in this book are but a few of the many that have shaped American high school life over the last century. The wins and losses on its pages have modified school dress codes, altered the content of textbooks, established the boundaries of free speech rights, and determined who would be allowed to learn (and to teach) at certain schools.

But the struggle continues.

It took more than 40 years of challenges by science teachers (and a U.S. Supreme Court case) to finally overturn laws like Tennessee's Butler Act. It was a tremendous victory for reserving science classrooms for science and keeping religion outside their doors. Since then, however, teachers, parents, and students have had to re-fight this battle over and over again—and not just in Louisiana and Kansas.

Likewise, a wave of protests and courtroom challenges in the 1950s and 1960s destroyed the legal underpinnings of racial segregation in the United States. However, government efforts to actually integrate schools have since been largely abandoned. By many measurements, American schools are more segregated today than they were in the 1960s.

Perhaps most clearly of all, for the last five decades, there has been a constant push from politicians to cut funding for public education (as well as other public services). These attempts have often demonized teachers, blaming them (and their students) for failing to operate at the same level, while offering them fewer and fewer resources. The results of this long-term trend have been exactly as one would predict.

The lesson here is simple. If students, parents, and teachers want quality schools, then they must fight for every last penny of education funding, and they must out-organize the for-profit education industry. Otherwise, K-12 schools will be underfunded and overcrowded, and college students will graduate with a lifetime's worth of student loan debt.

If students want schools that are safe, tolerant spaces where diverse people can exchange ideas in exciting and challenging ways, then they have to demand them.

The people in this book gave it their best shot.

Now it is your turn, dear readers.

To paraphrase a protest sign from one of the campaigns in this book...

...FIGHT FOR THE SCHOOLS YOU DESERVE.

ACKNOWLEDGMENTS

I have too many people to thank to do so properly, but I think that is probably a sign of a good life.

This book would not have happened without Joe Biel at Microcosm. Thanks, Joe. You do important work, and your enthusiasm for this project could not have been better timed. Thanks as well to Meggyn Pomerleau, whose wonderful artwork brings these stories to life.

Heartfelt thanks to Mark Rudd, for writing the book's foreword and for being a supportive and wise friend for the last several years.

Fittingly, I also owe an immense debt of gratitude to many great teachers, including Joe Austin, Rob Smith, Rachel Ida Buff, Steve Meyer, Aims McGuinness, Michael Gordon, Steven Fuller, and Alon Raab, among others. With the book's subject in mind, I am especially grateful to Steve Garrison, Michael Gray, and Trudy Jennings, who I've only recently realized were important allies when I (mistakenly) thought I might have to take on the world by myself.

Thanks as well to my many wonderful students at Del Mar, Gregory-Portland, and UW-Milwaukee, for teaching me, inspiring me, and assuring me that if the world is in the hands of their generation, we've got at least a fighting chance.

I would also like to thank my friends and family. You are too many to list, but you know who you are. Hopefully, I will see you all very soon.

Writing this book has made me particularly thankful for punk rock—the community, not just the music. Young people need a space, and that was mine. It relied on the efforts of lots of people. Thanks, people.

Above all, thanks to my friend, partner, and patient editor, Beth Robinson. Beth, now that I'm done writing this, I promise to play the Footloose soundtrack slightly less often. Well, maybe not promise...

Go get 'em!

SOURCES

Nearly all of the stories in this book were pulled from newspapers and other media accounts, including those presented in, on, and by:

101 KXL News, ABC News, Actipedia, Alamedan, Associated Press, *Atchison Daily Globe, Atlanta Journal-Constitution, Baltimore Sun, Bangor Daily News, Bleacher Report*, Brick City Live, *Bridgeport Post, Brooklyn Daily Eagle, Brown Daily Herald, Calhoun Times, Carbondale, Free Press*, CBS News, *Chattanooga Times Free Press, Chicago Bulletin, Chicago Tribune, Christian Science Monitor*, CNN, *Connecticut Post, Daily Independent, Daily Reporter, DCist, Democracy Now!, Deseret News, Dubois County Daily Herald, Education Week*, ESPN, *Eugene Register-Guard, Evening Independent, Evening Times*, Fox 4 News, *Freeport Journal-Standard, Fresno Bee, Guardian, Hale Sentinel, Huffington Post, Idaho Falls Post, Indian Country Today, Inside Higher Ed, Intelligencer Journal, Jacksonville Daily Journal*, KCET News, Kentucky New Era, KHOU News, *Kingsport News, Kingsport Times*, KIRO Radio, KITV NEWS, KOIN 6 News, *Kokomo Tribune*, KTEM News Radio, *Lewiston Evening Journal, Lewiston Sun Journal, Lock Haven Express, Lodi News-Sentinel, Lowell Sun, Marin Independent Journal, Maryland Gazette, Mason City Globe-Gazette*, Mic.com, Michigan Live, *Milwaukee Journal Sentinel, Minneapolis Tribune, Mt. Vernon Register-News*, NBC News, *New York Times, New York Tribune*, Oregon Public Broadcasting, *Oregonian*, PBS, People, *Perth Sunday Times, Post and Courier, Press-Telegram, Providence Journal*, Raw Story, Record-Argus, Redlands Daily Facts, RI NPR, Salon.com, *Salt Lake Tribune, San Bernardino Daily Sun, San Jose Mercury News, Sarasota Herald-Tribune*, sdnews.com, Seacoastonline, *Seattle Post-Intelligencer, Seattle Times, Sedalia Democrat, Simpson's Leader-Times*, Simsbury News, *Spartanburg Herald-Journal, Spokesman Review, Statesman Journal, Stranger, Sunday News and Tribune, Time, Troy Record, Tuscaloosa News, Ukiahi Daily Journal, Vidette-Messenger, Virginian-Pilot, Washington Post, Winston-Salem Journal*, 7 News Denver, *Denver Post, and U.S. News & World Report*, and WPRI News.

The book also draws on the work of the American Civil Liberties Union of Oregon, Advocates for Youth, BlackPast.org, the Brooklyn Public Library, the Chicago History Museum, Eagle Scouts Returning Our Badges, the Global Nonviolent Action Database, HistoricPatterson.org, the International Civil Rights Center and Museum, MarketingCharts, MeatlessMonday.com, the National Education Policy Center, the New York Civil Liberties Union, NoMoreMoney.org, Norfolk Public Schools, San Diego Unified School District, Seattle Public Schools, Siskiyou County Online, the Smithsonian Institute, the Southern Poverty Law Center, the Student Press Law Center, the Student-Farmworker Alliance, and Youth Empowered in the Struggle— and some occasional guidance from Wikipedia.

Material on the relationships between high school and college activists in the 1960s (from the introduction), the textile workers of Lowell, and American Indian boarding schools was taken, respectively, from Gael Graham's *Young Activists* (Northern Illinois University Press, 2006), Philip Foner's *History of the Labor Movement in the United States* (International Publishers Company, 1947), and Brenda Child's *Boarding School Seasons* (University of Nebraska Press, 2000).

SUBSCRIBE TO EVERYTHING WE PUBLISH!

Do you love what Microcosm publishes?

Do you want us to publish more great stuff?

Would you like to receive each new title as it's published?

Subscribe as a BFF to our new titles and we'll mail them all to you as they are released!

$10-30/mo, pay what you can afford. Include your t-shirt size and month/date of birthday for a possible surprise! Subscription begins the month after it is purchased.

microcosmpublishing.com/bff

...AND HELP US GROW YOUR SMALL WORLD!